2271.

Publications of the

MINNESOTA HISTORICAL SOCIETY

Russell W. Fridley, *Editor and Director*
June Drenning Holmquist, *Associate Editor*

MINNESOTA HISTORIC SITES PAMPHLET SERIES NO. 2

A HISTORY TOUR

of 50

TWIN CITY LANDMARKS

By Sue E. Holbert and June D. Holmquist

MINNESOTA HISTORICAL SOCIETY · ST. PAUL · 1966

Introduction

THIS PAMPHLET is the second in a new series of publications intended to illuminate historic places in Minnesota. Issued by the Minnesota Historical Society as a part of Minnesota's Natural Resources Program, this booklet is addressed to the growing band of young and old adventurers who enjoy seeking out the byways of history.

The first pamphlet in the series dealt in detail with *The Story of Fort Snelling*, the birthplace of Minnesota, and this — the second — fittingly suggests a tour of some remaining landmarks in the state's two principal cities, both of which were founded by settlers from the old fort.

Minnesota's two largest cities — Minneapolis and St. Paul — are nonidentical twins. St. Paul is the older of the pair and the capital of the state; Minneapolis is younger, larger, and faster growing. Residents and visitors will find in these pages a cross section of fifty fascinating sites that have helped to make the Twin Cities what they are today.

Forty-four of the landmarks selected for inclusion are within the limits of the two cities; six lie on the suburban perimeters. Maps are provided to guide visitors easily from one landmark to the next. The first section of the booklet covers St. Paul, the second Minneapolis, and the third the Fort Snelling–Mendota area. Most of the sites are illustrated. Unless otherwise noted, the pictures are in the collections of the Minnesota Historical Society.

The authors, who are both on the society's publications department staff, were guided by three basic criteria in selecting these sites. (1) The buildings, statues, parks, and markers have significance and interest for the history of the region or were associated with persons and events that had a distinct impact on the development of the nation, the state, or the city. (2) There must be some visible remains–a structure, ruins, or an identifying marker. (3) A number of structures of architectural merit have been included, but this was not a primary consideration in their selection.

Most of the landmarks date from the nineteenth century. A few, like Mounds Park in St. Paul, reach back through the ages to early man. Others point to the Sioux and Chippewa, who lived in the area when the white man arrived. Still others document the development of Minnesota from frontier territory to modern commonwealth. Many have been the homes of pioneers — fur traders, missionaries, statesmen, authors, and businessmen. In these pages, too, you will find explorers, legendary figures like Hiawatha, soldiers like Josias R. King, parks and pioneer mills, bridges, and even a railroad locomotive. All have played a part in the story of Minnesota.

St. Paul and Minneapolis, Minnesota's largest metropolitan center, owe their existence to the Mississippi River. St. Paul, located at the head of practical navigation on the river, became a popular port of call for steamboats in the 1840s. When Minnesota Territory was created in 1849, the bustling settlement became the capital city and the leading commercial center of the state.

In the 1860s, when railroads reached Minnesota, vigorous St. Paul became the headquarters of lines leading to Lake Superior, to southern Minnesota, and to connections with eastern systems. Before the city was thirty years old it could, and did, boast that it was the railroad and political capital of Minnesota and the commercial emporium of the Northwest.

Minneapolis, nine miles upstream from St. Paul, got a later start. It owes its existence to the Falls of St. Anthony, the only major waterfall in the Mississippi River. In the early years, the site was part of the Fort Snelling military reservation. Not until 1837 could settlers take up land there, and then only the east bank of the falls was open to them. Pioneers who built their homes on the east shore named their town St. Anthony in honor of the falls. In the early 1850s, when the military reservation was further reduced and the land on the west bank was opened to settlement, a second town grew up at the cataract. Called Minneapolis, it was linked to St. Anthony by a beautiful suspension bridge. In 1872 the towns united under the name Minneapolis to become the largest city in Minnesota.

The Falls of St. Anthony generated power for saw and flour mills that made the city known throughout the nation. Minneapolis had commercial ambitions, too. Competing with St. Paul for railroads and the trade of the Northwest, it became a wholesaling as well as a manufacturing center. Although each of the cities predicted that it would some day absorb the other, both prospered. Today St. Paul and Minneapolis are similar in economy and urban growth but different in their social and political traditions.

Cities are usually careless about their historic places, and St. Paul and Minneapolis are no exceptions. Visitors will find the sites listed in this book in various stages of development — from Carver's Cave, which has been substantially destroyed, to the Alexander Ramsey House, the Victorian mansion of the territory's first governor, which has been well preserved and is open to the public. The work of both public and private organizations and the interest of individual citizens have been important factors in the preservation of the still-existing landmarks described in this booklet.

In spite of, or perhaps because of, its greater age, St. Paul is better represented by historic structures and markers than is Minneapolis. Nevertheless an even larger book could be written about the equally interesting sites which have been destroyed in both cities. A city seldom pays much attention to its heritage until it has permitted many of its landmarks to be erased. And the pace of destruction is accelerating with the onslaught of urban renewal and freeways. So here is a tour of fifty sites that have figured prominently in Minnesota history — sites that I urge you to visit on a Sunday ramble before it is too late and many of them fall victim to the changing landscape of the twentieth century.

St. Paul, Minnesota
July 15, 1966

RUSSELL W. FRIDLEY, Director
Minnesota Historical Society

Contents

Fort Snelling—Mendota Historic Sites

Maps

25 ST. PAUL LANDMARKS

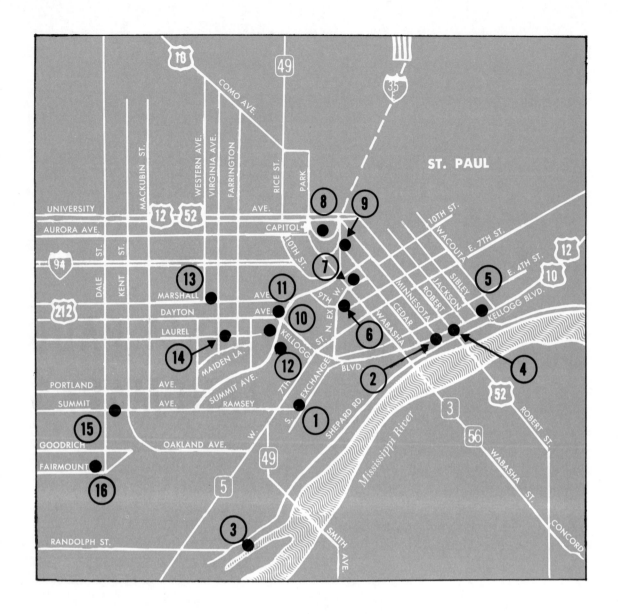

Downtown St. Paul Area

THIS HOUSE is both historically and architecturally significant. It was built between 1868 and 1872 in the then fashionable Irvine Park section of St. Paul by Alexander Ramsey, a Pennsylvanian who was appointed the first governor of Minnesota Territory in 1849 and who served his adopted state until his death in 1903.

The man who built this house and lived in it until his death was one of the founders of Minnesota. A member of the Whig and later of the Republican party, he held more high offices during his lifetime than any other Minnesotan. In addition to being the first governor of Minnesota Territory, Ramsey became the second governor of the state in 1859, and he was re-elected in 1861. He served in the United States Senate from 1863 to 1875, and was secretary of war and secretary of the navy in the cabinet of President Rutherford B. Hayes (1879–81). President Hayes visited this house twice. As governor of Minnesota during the Civil War, Ramsey had the further distinction of being the first northern governor to offer troops for the Union army in 1861.

Ramsey's handsome sixteen-room, three-story

1 | Alexander Ramsey House

265 South Exchange Street

"Mansion House," constructed of native limestone, is considered one of the best remaining examples in the state of the mid-Victorian period. Designed by St. Paul architect Monroe Sheire, it has three verandas and a mansard roof — a roof with four steep sides broken by former windows. The mansard style originated in France. It became popular in the United States after the mid-nineteenth century and went out of fashion in the mid-1870s soon after the Ramsey House was completed.

Few structural changes were made in the home during the ninety-two years the family lived there. Architectural details, Victorian fur-

WHEN Alexander Ramsey completed this house in 1872, cows still roamed in Irvine Park less than a block away. In the next decade the area became one of the city's most exclusive residential districts. Photograph by Eugene D. Becker, 1965.

nishings, and many personal belongings of Ramsey and his family contribute to its interest.

The house was willed to the Minnesota Historical Society in 1964 by Ramsey's granddaughters, Anna E. and Laura Furness. It is open to the public weekdays (except Wednesdays) from 10:00 A.M. to noon and from 1:00 P.M. to 4:00 P.M. On Saturdays and Sundays the hours are from 2:00 P.M. to 5:00 P.M. There is a small admission fee. Reservations are required for group tours. For information call or write the Minnesota Historical Society.

2 | Chapel of St. Paul Marker

Kellogg Boulevard at the foot of Minnesota Street

THE ERECTION of a humble log chapel on this site overlooking the Mississippi River was one of the most important events in the history of St. Paul, for the chapel became the nucleus around which the city developed.

The Chapel of St. Paul was built by Father Lucien Galtier and a dozen or so Catholic families in 1841. The French priest had been sent to the Minnesota country only a year before to open a mission. He began his work at Mendota, but he often crossed the river to conduct services in the shanties of would-be settlers who had been evicted from the Fort Snelling military

reservation in 1840. After being told that they could not take up land near the fort, a number of these settlers moved a short distance downriver and clustered about the cabin of a whisky seller named Pierre "Pig's Eye" Parrant.

At first the new settlement was called Pig's Eye, but after the chapel was built it became known as St. Paul's Landing, later as St. Paul's, and eventually as St. Paul.

Father Galtier had wisely chosen a site that could be used as a steamboat landing, and within a decade the town growing up about the chapel became the capital of Minnesota Territory and the head of navigation on the Mississippi River.

The chapel was constructed of red and white oak logs held together with wooden pins. In later years Father Galtier was often asked to describe how it was built. He said, "The roof was made of steeply slanting, bark-covered slabs, surmounted by a wooden cross." If the labor and materials needed to build it had not been volunteered by the parishioners, the whole structure would have represented a cash outlay of $65. The building was 25 feet long, 18 feet wide, and 10 feet high. Tamarack had been used for the rafters, pews, and floor. In 1847 Father Augustin Ravoux, who succeeded Father Galtier, built a twenty-foot addition, but the congregation had already outgrown its first home.

In 1851 four Sisters of St. Joseph began teaching school in the Chapel of St. Paul. After a new school was built in 1852 (see no. 13), they continued to use the log building as a chapel. During an outbreak of cholera in 1854, the sisters

THIS OIL of the Chapel of St. Paul was painted by Robert O. Sweeny, a St. Paul druggist, in 1852.

The original is in the picture collection of the Minnesota Historical Society.

converted the little church into a temporary infirmary where they cared for the sick.

The chapel was torn down in the late 1850s. Bishop Thomas L. Grace, who planned to rebuild it, had the logs taken to the grounds of the new St. Joseph's Academy. There they were burned by workmen who were unaware of the plans to restore the pioneer church. A granite boulder bearing commemorative tablets now marks the chapel's original location.

FOUNTAIN CAVE was one of the scenic sights of early St. Paul. This picture of it appeared on a postcard about 1868.

3 | Fountain Cave Marker

Shepard Road near Randolph Avenue

AT A SCENIC OVERLOOK on Shepard Road on the banks of the Mississippi River is a tablet describing Fountain Cave, an early landmark which is no longer visible. Through the years debris accumulated to block the entrance, and construc-

tion of a highway in the early 1960s made it necessary to fill in most of the ravine.

The cave was known as early as 1811 and was visited by explorer Stephen H. Long in 1817. Long described it as "far more curious & interesting" than Carver's Cave (*see no. 17*) and said: "To beautify and embellish the scene, a fine chrystal stream flows thro' the cavern, & cheers the lonesome dark retreat with its enlivening murmurs." It attracted the attention of Henry R. Schoolcraft in 1820 and of the distinguished French scientist, Joseph N. Nicollet, in 1837. These men set forth its wonders in their journals, and tourists from many lands visited it over the years.

Fountain Cave is associated with St. Paul's beginnings, for it was in a ravine near the cave that Pierre "Pig's Eye" Parrant in 1838 erected the small saloon which was the first building on the site of present-day St. Paul. One early writer gave a possibly exaggerated account of "the drunken Indian hordes, and the inebriate white men" who frequented "Pig's-Eye Pandemonium." The same author commented that Parrant mysteriously disappeared one day, adding, "Very few cared to know why he went, and some were glad that he had really gone."

4 | Jacob Fahlstrom Marker

Kellogg Boulevard near Robert Street

IN JUNE, 1948, Prince Bertil of Sweden took part in ceremonies dedicating this marker in memory of Jacob Fahlstrom,* the first Swede to reach what is now Minnesota.

Fahlstrom, who has been called "the harbinger of Swedish immigration to Minnesota," had a checkered career which is difficult to trace. Born in Stockholm in 1793 or 1795, he left home at an early age and somehow made his way to England. There he was directed to Lord Selkirk, who was raising a company of men to go to his

*The name is spelled in various ways: Falstrom, Fahlström, Fulstrom, Folstrom, Fölstrom.

colony on the Red River near present-day Winnipeg. Young Fahlstrom accompanied the group. He is known to have been at the Selkirk settlement in 1812.

Subsequently he became a fur trader in the employ of the Hudson's Bay Company and perhaps the American Fur Company. Trading with the Chippewa in the Lake Superior region, he is said to have learned certain Indian dialects, a little English, and the French-Canadian patois. In 1823 he married Margaret Bonga, the daughter of a prominent Negro fur trader and a Chippewa woman.

Sometime before 1831 the Swede and his wife moved to Fort Snelling, where he was employed by Indian agent Major Lawrence Taliaferro. Fahlstrom also carried the mail on foot through the wild, unpeopled region between Fort Snelling and Fort Crawford at Prairie du Chien in what is now Wisconsin.

After the settlers were evicted from the Fort Snelling military reservation in 1840, the Fahlstroms and their many children moved to a farm near what is now Afton in Washington County.

Late in the 1830s the Swede and his wife were converted to Methodism at the Sioux mission near Kaposia (*see no. 20*). Fahlstrom's conversion was, in the opinion of its founder, the mission's only noteworthy achievement while at that location.

After the 1830s Jacob Fahlstrom devoted himself to the cause of religion. He was given a license to preach and work among the Indians. He acted as guide and interpreter for other Methodist missionaries, and in 1853 he served at a mission to the Mille Lacs Chippewa.

When Minnesota Territory was established in 1849, the vanguard of a vast host of Swedish immigrants began to flock to Minnesota. Fahlstrom conducted prayer meetings in the homes of his countrymen. He died on his Washington County farm in 1859.

THE "WILLIAM CROOKS," described on page 7, was the first iron horse in Minnesota. It ushered in a new era of transportation. This photograph was taken by M. C. Tuttle of St. Paul about 1864.

5 | The "William Crooks"

On display in the lobby of the St. Paul Union Depot, 214 East Fourth Street

A HEADLINE in the *St. Paul Pioneer and Democrat* of September 20, 1861, proclaimed "the first railroad trip in Minnesota." The day before, the "fine locomotive 'Wm. Crooks'" had puffed and chugged its way "at a rapid rate" for about two hundred yards, and then returned to the banks of the Mississippi.

It was nine months later — on July 2, 1862 — that regular service began on the ten-mile line from St. Paul to St. Anthony (now part of Minneapolis). Four days earlier, the "William Crooks" had carried "excited excursionists" between the two cities. The newspapers, hailing the coming of the iron horse to Minnesota, called the trip "the first link in the great chain of railroads which will, in the course of a few years, spread all over this State."

In the excursion party were two men who were instrumental in putting the railroad into operation: Edmund Rice, president of the St. Paul and Pacific Railway (eventually the Great Northern), and William Crooks, chief engineer, for whom the engine was named. Another dignitary in the crowd was Governor Alexander Ramsey.

The "William Crooks" was assembled, largely by hand, in New Jersey. From there it was shipped by rail to La Crosse, Wisconsin, where it was loaded on a barge and towed up the Mississippi, arriving in St. Paul on September 9, 1861. After the trial run on September 19, it was put into storage for the winter because the tracks to St. Anthony had not been completed.

The little twenty-five-ton engine burned wood. The tender held only two cords of wood; if the supply was depleted before the next woodpile was reached, the train stopped and any nearby fences were dismantled for fuel. The "William Crooks" had a top speed of sixty miles an hour, but it usually ran at only fifteen to twenty-five miles an hour.

The engine saw service until about 1900. In later years it burned coal and was used only for special trips. In 1908 it was brought out of retirement, polished up, and used to take passengers from St. Paul to Great Northern chairman James J. Hill's seventieth birthday party at Lake Minnetonka.

The old engine was kept in running condition until it was placed on display in the Union Depot in 1954. It went to the Baltimore Fair of the Iron Horse in 1927, the New York World's Fair in 1939, and the Chicago Railroad Fair in 1948. In 1962, the centenary of railroading in Minnesota, the Great Northern Railway presented the venerable locomotive to the Minnesota Historical Society.

6 | Assumption Church

51 West Ninth Street

THE SOARING 210-foot twin towers of Assumption Church in downtown St. Paul are a familiar landmark. The beautiful German Romanesque revival structure was built of local limestone between 1869 and 1873 by a German Catholic parish which was then the largest in the state.

The pastor, Father Clement Staub, decided that the first Assumption Church, which had been in use since 1856, should be replaced by a handsome stone edifice of German design. He engaged Joseph Reidl, court architect for the ruling Wittelsbach family of Bavaria, to draw plans for the church. Reidl patterned it after the famous Ludwigskirche in Munich, but when his plans arrived in St. Paul, it was feared that they were too ambitious for the congregation's purse.

Father Staub persisted, and the church was dedicated in October, 1874. Many dignitaries and one of the largest crowds in St. Paul's history up to that time attended the ceremonies, but the new church was criticized as being too plain for Victorian tastes.

Nearby at 68 Exchange Street is Assumption School erected by the congregation in 1864.

ALTHOUGH the surrounding area has changed, Assumption Church looks today just as it did when this photograph was taken about 1895.

7 | Site of First and Second Minnesota Capitols

Block bounded by Tenth, Cedar, Exchange, and Wabasha Streets

WHEN MINNESOTA was organized as a territory in 1849, Congress specified that the first legislature should meet in St. Paul. Although several disputes later raged over the location of the capital, it has remained in St. Paul since that time.

The city at the head of steamboat navigation on the Mississippi River was officially designated as the capital by the legislature in 1851, but not until 1853 was the first capitol building erected. In that year a plain, two-story statehouse with a cupola on top was built at Tenth and Wabasha; it was destroyed by fire in 1881.

A larger and more elaborate structure was

THIS STRUCTURE served as the Minnesota capitol from 1853 to 1881 during territorial and early statehood days. At first, it was surrounded by mud streets and frame houses.

A MORE imposing capitol was erected on the site of the first one in 1883, but Minnesota soon outgrew its second statehouse.

erected on the same site in 1883. It served as the capitol of the growing state until the present building was completed in 1904. The second capitol, a red brick building with a lofty tower, was razed in 1938.

The St. Paul Art and Science Center now occupies the site where Minnesota's first two capitols stood.

8 | Minnesota State Capitol

Cedar Street and Aurora Avenue

THIS ELABORATE marble and granite structure is the third Minnesota statehouse. Ground was broken for it in 1896, but the cornerstone was not laid until two years later. Six years were then required to build it, and it was completed in 1904 at a cost of about $4,500,000. Samuel R. Van Sant was the first chief executive to occupy the present capitol; the legislature has met there since 1905.

The building was designed in the Italian Renaissance tradition by Cass Gilbert of St. Paul. One of the outstanding architects of his day, Gilbert also planned the United States Supreme Court Building in Washington, D.C., and many other famous structures.

The Minnesota Capitol is 434 feet long, 229 feet wide, and 223 feet high to the top of the dome. The quadriga of gold leaf above the main entrance is composed of six statues representing the virtues of Wisdom, Courage, Bounty, Truth, Integrity, and Prudence that support the progress of the state. These are the work of Daniel Chester French, an American sculptor who was also responsible for the seated statue of Abraham Lincoln in the Lincoln Memorial in Washington.

Guided tours of the building are given Mondays through Fridays. Reservations are required for groups.

THE PRESENT Minnesota State Capitol, which was completed in 1904, is framed by the arch of the Cedar Street overpass on University Avenue in this unusual view photographed by Becker in 1966.

9 | Minnesota Historical Society Building and Museum

690 Cedar Street

THE MINNESOTA HISTORICAL SOCIETY is the oldest institution in the state. It is in fact older than the state, for it was chartered by the first territorial legislature a few months after Minnesota Territory was established in 1849. Since that time the society has worked to collect, preserve, and interpret the history of the state and the area. The Historical Building, the organization's first permanent home, was completed in 1917. It is located immediately southeast of the State Capitol.

The society has excellent collections of books, pictures, manuscripts, and newspapers relating to the region, as well as a museum that depicts the state's development in exhibits on Indians, the fur trade, pioneer life, and more recent history.

The museum on the third floor is open to the public from 8:30 A.M. to 5:00 P.M. weekdays, from 10:00 A.M. to 4:00 P.M. Saturdays, and from 2:00 to 5:00 P.M. Sundays. Reservations must be made for guided group tours.

The Minnesota Historical Society also owns or operates museums and historic sites throughout the state. More information on these activities, and details of tours, hours, and fees, may be obtained by calling the society at its building in St. Paul.

Archaeological exploration of sites and underwater archaeology are among other aspects of the organization's work. The restoration of Old Fort Snelling is one of its current projects (*see no. 48*).

Membership in the society is open to all who are interested in the area's history.

THE Minnesota Historical Building was constructed of local stone. The walls are of gray granite from Sauk Rapids, the staircases of Kasota marble, and the entrance hall of stone from Frontenac. The building, completed in 1917, was designed by Clarence H. Johnston. Photograph by Becker, 1966.

10 | Cathedral of St. Paul

Summit, Dayton, and Selby Avenues

THE CORNERSTONE of this impressive cathedral, on a superb site overlooking the city, was laid in 1907. The need for such a church to serve the growing archdiocese of St. Paul had been envisioned by Archbishop John Ireland three years before. Ireland, who was "never one to do things in a small way," planned for a "great cathedral," symbolizing the strength of Catholicism in the upper Midwest. In 1905 before work on the cathedral got under way the archbishop estimated that "simply to fit" it "for occupancy" would cost "at least one million dollars."

Ireland said the first mass in the still unfinished church on Palm Sunday, 1915. He died in 1918, having lived to see his grand design take shape and the exterior completed. The interior was gradually finished over the years between

THIRTY THOUSAND LAYMEN marched in the "greatest" parade in the "history of the West" in ceremonies marking the laying of the cornerstone for the Cathedral of St. Paul on June 2, 1907. Photograph by Becker, 1966.

11

1915 and 1941, although certain details of the original plan still remain to be executed.

The cathedral was designed by Emmanuel L. Masqueray, an architect who immigrated to the United States from France about 1881. With Archbishop Ireland's active encouragement, he worked out a plan for the church which followed the main lines of Michelangelo's design for St. Peter's Cathedral in Rome.

The structure, built of St. Cloud granite, can seat 4,000 people. Its dome is 186 feet high and has a diameter of 96 feet. The over-all height of the cathedral is 307 feet. The interior decoration is lavish neo-baroque.

The first Catholic church in St. Paul was a crude log chapel erected in 1841 (*see no. 2*). Two other structures served the diocese before the present cathedral was erected.

11 | Josias R. King Statue

Summit Park below the Cathedral of St. Paul

JOSIAS R. KING was the "first man to volunteer" for service in the Union army of the Civil War. He gained this distinction by being the initial recruit for the First Minnesota, which the inscription at the base of this statue notes was the "first regiment tendered the government for the suppression of the rebellion." The monument also honors "the memory of the Union soldiers and sailors of the war."

The statue, which is three times life size, depicts King in the full-dress uniform of a Union soldier. King posed for it and was among the four thousand people who attended the ceremonies dedicating the statue on November 21, 1903.

The sculptor was John K. Daniels, a Norwegian who came to America at the age of nine and lived most of his life in the Twin Cities. Other St. Paul examples of Daniels' work include the statues of Knute Nelson (opposite the State Capitol), Leif Ericson (opposite the State Office Building), and "Earthbound" (in front of the Veterans Service Building).

THE HOUSE built for James J. Hill included a billiard room, a music room, a large library, and a sky-lighted art gallery. The photograph was taken in the 1890s.

12 | James J. Hill House

240 Summit Avenue

JAMES J. HILL, the "Empire Builder" of railroads in the Northwest, began the construction of this four-story red sandstone house at the height of his career in 1889. He moved into it with his wife and eight of his ten children in 1891, when it was completed at a cost of about $200,000.

The house, which became well known as a gracious family home and a show place for Hill's famous art collection, was designed by Peabody and Stearns of Boston in a style sometimes called "heavy Richardson Romanesque" with high chimneys, slate roofs, many dormers, and a porté-cochere with semicircular arches. When it was built, it was thought to be the most successful and elaborate, as well as the largest, residence of this style in the state.

The interior was lavishly finished with polished and carved woods and enormous fireplaces. Twelve stained glass windows dominated the stairway landing, and the house contained a two-story art gallery, the skylights of which are still visible from the exterior. Hill displayed what has been called "the first important private collection of paintings and sculpture in Minnesota."

A complex man of many interests, Hill died in 1919 after a long and successful career as a railroad executive and financier. As the guiding genius of the Great Northern Railway, he also had at times large interests in the Canadian Pacific, the Northern Pacific, and the Chicago, Burlington, and Quincy railroads.

Nine years after Hill's death, the house was presented to the Catholic archdiocese of St. Paul by four of his daughters. The exterior remains unchanged, but the interior has been remodeled. In 1961 the National Park Service designated the building a National Historic Landmark, one of only four in the state. It is still owned by the archdiocese. *It is not open to the public.*

THE WESTERNMOST WING (at left) of St. Joseph's Academy, completed in 1863, is thought to be the oldest remaining Catholic schoolhouse in the state. Before additions were made to the north and east, orchards and gardens were cultivated on the land. Photograph by A. F. Raymond, 1936.

13 | St. Joseph's Academy

Western and Marshall Avenues

THE NOW FLOURISHING WORK of the Sisters of St. Joseph of Carondelet in Minnesota began in 1851 when four nuns arrived in St. Paul on a snowy November night. Ice was forming in the river as the steamboat that had carried them up the Mississippi from their headquarters in St. Louis docked at the tiny capital of Minnesota Territory.

One of the French sisters left a description of her arrival. She wrote: "We then were shown Our New home, a small fram[e] Shanty on the Riverbank. We took our first meal, Supper . . . in the . . . Old log Church. We had difficulty to get Water enough to make our tea as there was but one Well in the town and that was locked up."

Soon after they arrived the sisters opened "a ladies' seminary," known as St. Joseph's Academy, in the little log chapel of St. Paul (*see no. 2*). The following year a two-story brick schoolhouse was erected for the sisters near the chapel. When they moved into the new building, in the

fall of 1852, the nuns had 87 pupils, including 17 boarding students. The sisters gave instruction in reading, writing, arithmetic, grammar, geography, history, astronomy, chemistry, botany, literature, music, and all kinds of needlework.

A year later, at the urging of Bishop Joseph Cretin, the construction of St. Joseph's Hospital — the first institution of its kind in Minnesota — was begun at Ninth and Exchange streets. The hospital, which was completed in 1854, was staffed by the sisters and cared not only for the poor but also for orphaned children. Paying patients, of whom there were very few, were charged eight dollars a week. For a time the sisters also used the new building as an academy and novitiate. (The present hospital is located on the site of this pioneer structure. The oldest remaining building dates from 1878. The hospital and the academy became entirely separate in 1863.)

By the 1860s the sisters felt that a new school building was needed to house their growing classes. As a result, the imposing yellow limestone structure which still stands at what is now Western and Marshall avenues was completed in 1863. It is preserved in excellent condition as the westernmost wing of the present school. The wing is thought to be the oldest remaining Catholic schoolhouse in the state. A marker calling attention to the academy's history was erected on the grounds in 1966 by the St. Paul City Planning Board.

The first floor contained parlors, a library–music room, and a playroom for the students. The second floor had a chapel and classrooms. Additional classrooms and dormitories were on the third floor.

When the academy opened it had three teachers. It was located so far from the residential sections of St. Paul that most of the pupils boarded until about 1870, when transportation improved.

14 | F. Scott Fitzgerald Birthplace

481 Laurel Avenue

ON THE AFTERNOON of September 24, 1896, St. Paul's most famous author was born in this building, once known as the San Mateo Flats.

Fitzgerald, whose father was a furniture dealer at that time, lived here with his family until 1898. Economic reversals occasioned a move to Buffalo, New York, but by 1908 the Fitzgeralds returned to St. Paul, where Scott's parents remained for the rest of their lives.

From 1908 until 1919 — when he was not away at school or in the army — the budding author lived on or near Summit Avenue, "St. Paul's show street." Fitzgerald's first published work (1909) was written in the capital city and appeared in *Now and Then*, a literary magazine he helped to establish at the St. Paul Academy.

This building, which still contains apartments, *is not open to the public.* It is probable that the porches on the front are a later addition, since they do not appear in views dating from the Fitzgeralds' residence in the 1890s.

ON A September afternoon in 1896 a strapping baby, weighing ten pounds, six ounces, was born in this apartment house. He was christened Francis Scott Key Fitzgerald. Photograph by Becker, 1964.

15 | F. Scott Fitzgerald Residence

599 Summit Avenue

FITZGERALD, who was always on the move, lived briefly at 599 Summit Avenue in 1919. He described it as "a house below the average on a street above the average." Here he rewrote **This Side of Paradise**. Photograph by Becker, 1964.

IN THIS HOUSE on Summit Avenue the novelist who successfully portrayed the jazz age of the 1920s completed the writing of his first book, *This Side of Paradise*, during the summer of 1919. Fitzgerald once called Summit Avenue "a museum of American architectural failures," but the street was for him a symbol of the social success he never quite attained, and, as such, it continued to fascinate him long after he left St. Paul.

The house is one of a group of eight attached dwellings called Summit Terrace, which was recommended in 1964 for a historic marker by the Historic Sites Committee of the St. Paul City Planning Board because of its unusual architecture as well as its relationship to Fitzgerald's career.

This is a private residence; *it is not open to the public.*

16 | Frank B. Kellogg House

633 Fairmount Avenue

THE INTERNATIONALLY KNOWN Minnesota diplomat of the 1920s, Frank B. Kellogg, began to build this house near Summit Avenue in 1889, two years after he moved to St. Paul from Rochester, Minnesota. At that time, Kellogg was a practicing attorney in the St. Paul firm of Davis, Kellogg, and Severance, where he soon gained national prominence as a trust-busting lawyer.

From 1917 to 1923 he represented Minnesota in the United States Senate, and was a leading "mild reservationist" in Senate debates over the League of Nations. In 1921 and 1922 he acted

THE RICHARDSONIAN-STYLE home built for Frank B. Kellogg has rounded forms and flowing lines. Photograph by Truman W. Ingersoll in the 1890s.

15

as spokesman for the Republican majority on the important Senate foreign relations committee when it considered the treaties to limit armaments after World War I. As ambassador to England from 1923 to 1925, he also played an important role in the negotiation of the Dawes plan for economic reparations.

From 1925 to 1929 Kellogg served as secretary of state in the cabinet of President Calvin Coolidge. While secretary of state, he was a key figure in the drafting of the famous Pact of Paris, the so-called Kellogg–Briand pact to outlaw war, which was signed on August 27, 1928. For his work on the agreement, he received the Nobel Peace Prize in 1929. His public career continued in the 1930s when he served for five years as a judge on the World Court.

He lived in this house of pink stone and wood shingles off and on over the years from 1889 until his death in 1937 at the age of eighty-one.

The house is a private residence; *it is not open to the public.*

17 | Carver's Cave Marker

Mounds Boulevard between Plum and Cherry Streets

ONE OF THE MEN who explored the Minnesota area under the British flag was Captain Jonathan Carver. He traveled a short distance up the Minnesota and Mississippi rivers in 1766 in search of a Northwest Passage to the Pacific. Although he failed to find it, Carver achieved a place in history by discovering the St. Paul cave that bears his name and by writing a book which brought the Minnesota country to the attention of European readers.

It was in the autumn of 1766 that Carver arrived at the present site of St. Paul and visited what he called "a remarkable cave" along the Mississippi River. He returned to the site the following spring to hold a council with the Sioux Indians.

Carver described the cave in the following words: "The Indians term it *Wakon-teebe*, that is the Dwelling of the Great Spirit. The entrance into it is about ten feet wide, the height of it five feet. The arch within is near fifteen feet high and about thirty feet broad. . . . About twenty feet from the entrance begins a lake, the water of which is transparent, and extends to an unsearchable distance. . . . I found in this cave many Indian hieroglyphicks, which appeared very ancient, for time had nearly covered them with moss. . . . They were cut in a rude manner upon the inside of the walls, which were com-

posed of a stone so extremely soft that it might be easily penetrated with a knife."

Eleven years later Carver published a book about his journey to Minnesota which became a best seller, and in the years that followed the cave was visited by other explorers — some of whom found its entrance blocked. After St. Paul was settled, Carver's Cave became a great tourist attraction.

In 1867 the Minnesota Historical Society commemorated the centenary of Carver's council

THE SUN reflects on the lake in the interior of Carver's Cave in this photograph taken by W. H. Illingworth about 1870.

16

with the Sioux by sponsoring a trip to the cave. The visitors paddled a boat around the interior lake and noted that the hieroglyphics were still visible on the walls. As late as 1879 an archaeologist reported that "there were plainly to be seen snakes, birds, men, animals, fish, and turtles" whose "antiquity . . . is great." Ten years later

these drawings had been ruined, and no copies of them are preserved.

The accumulation of debris and the construction of roads and railroads have long since made the cave inaccessible, but a marker stands at a wayside on Mounds Boulevard near the site of the famous landmark.

A FEW of the Indian burial mounds that still exist in the state are preserved in Mounds Park. Photograph taken in 1960.

18 | Mounds Park

Mounds Boulevard and Earl Street

"AT A LITTLE DISTANCE from this dreary cavern [Carver's Cave], is the burying place of several bands of the Naudowessie [Sioux] Indians; though these people have no fixed residence, living in tents, and abiding but a few months on one spot, yet they always bring the bones of their dead to this place." Thus Jonathan Carver in 1766 described the Indian graves that are now preserved in Mounds Park.

At least eighteen burial mounds were originally present in the area of the park, and nine-

teen more were found along Dayton's Bluff. Today six remain, and credit for preserving them belongs to Joseph A. Wheelock, a St. Paul journalist (editor of the St. Paul Pioneer Press for thirty years) and the creator of the city's park system.

Wheelock became president of the St. Paul Park Board in 1893. Before his connection with the board, the city had virtually no park system. During his years of devotion to the cause, Wheelock was responsible for the development of many of St. Paul's boulevards and parks. The land for Indian Mounds Park was obtained by him in long negotiations with the various owners.

Although few remain, more than ten thousand

burial mounds have been surveyed in the state. Those in St. Paul were first excavated in 1856 by Edward D. Neill, a St. Paul minister, historian, and secretary of the Minnesota Historical Society. Later Daniel A. Robertson worked on the mounds for the society, but it was Theodore H. Lewis who contributed the most to our knowledge of them in a series of investigations made from 1879 through 1883.

Burials of several types were found. Some were accompanied by objects; some were small bundle burials in the upper parts of mounds. Others contained bones placed in stone cists or log tombs, and one was a pit burial. One mound in the park area disclosed what Lewis called a "rare find" — the facial bones of a skull which had been covered with red clay, producing a death mask that revealed an image of the face.

Current archaeological opinion holds that the mounds do not belong to any single period; that they were built by different peoples beginning more than three thousand years ago and continuing through the succeeding centuries to the end of the prehistoric period.

19 | Battle of Kaposia Marker

At the entrance to Battle Creek Park, east of U.S. Highway 61

ONE OF THE LAST BATTLES between those implacable enemies, the Sioux and the Chippewa, took place in 1842 near a stream now called Battle Creek. The assault, which was part of the continuing warfare between the tribes, evidently was made by the Chippewa in retaliation for an unsuccessful Sioux attack the year before. In the earlier skirmish, the Kaposia Sioux had been defeated and two sons of Chief Big Thunder, or Little Crow IV, were killed.

In June, 1842, a party of Chippewa, numbering perhaps a hundred, went from the head of Lake St. Croix to a point opposite Little Crow's village of Kaposia (see no. 20). There they concealed themselves, planning to ambush any Sioux who happened to cross the stream. However, a scouting party of Chippewa shot and killed two Sioux women at work in a garden, prematurely revealing the presence of the Chippewa. The Sioux warriors hastily prepared for battle. Although they fell into the ambush and some were killed, the Sioux routed the Chippewa after several hours of fighting.

Accounts of the battle vary. The number of Sioux dead has been estimated at from eighteen to thirty, and the Chippewa loss from none to eight or nine. All versions agree that the Sioux loss was greater. Beengwa, a daughter of Chippewa Chief Augenosh of Sandy Lake, later related that the Chippewa held a victory dance, brandishing Sioux scalps.

The noise of the battle was heard in St. Paul and at Fort Snelling. Soldiers were dispatched from the fort, but they arrived after the action had ended.

Pioneer settler Auguste L. Larpenteur recalled many years later that even after he arrived in St. Paul in 1843, "the excitement in regard to this raid by the Ojibways [Chippewa] was the topic of almost every day's conversation, and an Ojibway Indian was supposed to be hidden behind every bush."

20 | Kaposia Indian Village Marker

1185 North Concord on Minnesota Highway 56 at the northern edge of South St. Paul

THIS MARKER recalls the Sioux Indian village of Kaposia, which from 1839 to 1852 was located in part of what is now South St. Paul.° Kaposia and

° As early as 1700 the French explorer Pierre Charles le Sueur mentioned the "Kapoja" band of the Sioux as living near the confluence of the Minnesota and Mississippi rivers. Although the exact site of the village changed several times during the next century and a half, it remained near the junction of the two rivers.

SETH EASTMAN, commandant at Fort Snelling at four different periods in the 1840s, painted many scenes of Indian life around the post. This water color, entitled "Dakotah Village," depicts Little Crow's Kaposia. The original is owned by the James Jerome Hill Reference Library, St. Paul.

its series of chiefs named Little Crow found their way into many of the accounts left by travelers and artists who journeyed up the Mississippi during those years.

A Frenchman who visited the Minnesota country in 1846 wrote: "Near the river bank, a little way up the side of the hill, one perceives a group of miserable huts, perhaps about thirty in number, forming the camps or village" of Little Crow. Above the village, which by then was on the west bank of the Mississippi, were groups of "aerial tombs" — the usual scaffold burials of the Sioux. Chief Little Crow, the Frenchman said, wore thirty-two or thirty-three feathers in his headdress, indicating the number of enemies he had killed. The writer also noted that Little Crow was married to three sisters with whom he "lived in peace."

When Ephraim S. Seymour saw Kaposia in 1849, he said that it was five miles below the small settlement of St. Paul, and that it had about forty lodges and a population of some three hundred Sioux. The Indians "were living in skin lodges, such as they use during the winter, and when traveling. These are formed of long, slender poles, stuck in the ground, in a circle of about eight feet in diameter, and united at the top, and covered with the raw hide of the buffalo, having the hair scraped off. They are in the form of a cone. . . . During the summer they live in bark houses, which are more spacious, and when seen from a distance, resemble . . . the log cabins of whites."

Artists Seth Eastman and Frank B. Mayer sketched the village, and various missionaries provided additional information about it. In the 1830s Samuel W. Pond, one of the famous pair of missionary brothers, helped the Kaposia band learn to plow. At the request of Little Crow, Dr. Thomas S. Williamson went to Kaposia in 1846 to set up a mission and school.

Chief Little Crow was a signer of the Treaty of Mendota in 1851. By that treaty and another negotiated two weeks earlier at Traverse des Sioux, the Sioux ceded most of southern Minnesota to the white men. In accordance with the provisions of those treaties, the band moved from Kaposia up the Minnesota River to a spot near present-day Redwood Falls.

The same chief was the leader of the disastrous Sioux Uprising of 1862. He was shot by white settlers the following year while picking berries. Records show that Little Crow had a total of six wives and twenty-two children.

19

21|Red Rock

At Newport, on U.S. Highways 10 and 61, on the grounds of the Newport Methodist Church

RED ROCK, a large granite boulder located on the bank of the Mississippi River at what is now Newport, was a well-known shrine of the Sioux. It later gave its name to a center of religious activities of the white men. The boulder was described by Samuel W. Pond, a missionary who served among the Sioux at Lake Calhoun in 1834. He wrote: "Stones were much worshipped . . . both with prayers and offerings" by these Indians. "They chose granite boulders and painted them red. There was a large sacred stone of this sort at Red Rock . . . and another between Kaposia and Mendota. Both were covered with votive offerings, such as tobacco, pieces of cloth, hatchets, knives, arrows, and other articles of small value."

Stephen R. Riggs, another missionary to the Sioux, explained: "Paint occupies an important place in all their worship. Scarlet or red is the religious color for sacrifices, while blue is used in many ceremonies. The use of paints," the Sioux believed, "was taught them by the gods. . . . No ceremony of worship is complete without the *wakań*, or sacred application of paint. The down of the female swan, colored scarlet, also forms a necessary part of sacrifices."

In the 1840s the Red Rock area became a center of Methodist missionary activity. There in 1839 the Reverend Benjamin T. Kavanaugh built a two-story log cabin. The upper floor served as a home for his family, the lower as a school for white and mixed-blood children. This structure — the oldest existing Methodist building in the state — as well as the sacred stone stand on the Newport Methodist Church grounds at Glen Road and Eleventh Avenue in Newport.

The famed Red Rock Camp Meeting held nearby ministered to thousands of settlers in the new country. The first one was held in 1869; by 1883 ten thousand people were reported in attendance at the campground on a single Sunday. With the passing of frontier conditions, camp meetings became less common, and attendance

IN THE FOREGROUND is the Red Rock of the Sioux. Behind it is the Newport Methodist Church. Photograph by Becker, 1966.

began to drop at Red Rock, although gatherings took place there until 1938.

22|Mattocks School

Snelling Avenue South between Montreal Avenue and Edgcumbe Road

WHEN Highland Park Senior High School began to use the historic structure known as Mattocks School for classes in 1965, it was the first time in thirty-six years that the building had been used for the purpose for which it was built. Originally located at what is today the intersection of Randolph and Snelling avenues, it is now on the high school grounds.

The one-room schoolhouse, which replaced an earlier wooden one, was constructed of local limestone at a cost of $1,800. It opened about 1871 as Webster School No. 9 of Reserve Township. In the late 1880s, when the township was annexed by St. Paul, the school became a part of the city system. It was then renamed to honor the Reverend John Mattocks, the city's first superintendent of schools who was also minister of the First Presbyterian Church from 1856 until his death in 1875.

Several years ago a St. Paul official recalled that in the early days "Children from many miles around walked to the school for their daily classes. The square bell tower had a clanging bell in it that could be heard around that wooded neighborhood."

The building was used for classes until 1929. From 1931 to 1962 it was maintained by Highland Park American Legion Post No. 215. Its preservation was ensured by removal to its present location in September, 1964. The exterior of the schoolhouse remains much as it was in 1871; the interior has been restored by the Historic Sites Committee of the St. Paul City Planning Board.

The man for whom the school was named was secretary of the school board and served as superintendent from about 1860 to 1872. Upon his death, the *St. Paul Daily Dispatch* stated: "Mr. Mattocks was early identified with every good movement and cause in our city. He gave much attention to educational matters. . . . During his term as Superintendent, he performed a vast amount of labor in organizing, controlling and directing our schools, at greatly inadequate compensation."

THE OLD AND THE NEW — Mattocks School and Highland Park Senior High School — blend harmoniously. Photograph by Becker, 1966.

Henry H. Sibley, who had been the state's first elected governor, lauded Mattocks for the "strong impetus in the right direction" he had given the schools. "And so kind and gentle, and withal firm, was he in the discharge of his duties, that teachers and pupils alike revered and loved him."

23 | Minnesota State Reform School Buildings

Concordia College Campus, between Interstate Highway 94 and Marshall Avenue at Hamline Avenue

THE "DEPLORABLE" ACTIONS and the alarming "depravity" of some early St. Paul youths led to the establishment of a juvenile reformatory in the 1860s. I. V. D. Heard, St. Paul city attorney, advanced the idea in 1865 because he was distressed over committing children to jail "where they were forced to pass their time in idleness,

or, still worse, in learning wickedness from the older criminals with whom they were confined."

A year later the state legislature appropriated $5,000 for a "House of Refuge," on the condition that St. Paul provide a matching sum. A tract called Burt Farm, then some miles outside the city, was purchased, and there in 1868 the institution — renamed the Minnesota State Reform School — opened. At that time the "entire school" consisted of one "poor little" girl.

John G. Riheldaffer, a Presbyterian minister who had been in charge of the respected St. Paul Female Seminary for ten years, became the first superintendent. He remained in that post until 1886. Four years later the school was moved to Red Wing; it is now called the State Training School for Boys.

THIS photograph of the Minnesota State Reform School was taken about 1875 by Ingersoll. At left is the building now called Old West; next to it is Old South. Two other structures have been razed.

The newspapers of the day praised the reform school. "It is evident," ran a typical comment, "that the boys are well cared for and under the gentle, but firm treatment of Dr. J. G. Riheldaffer, bid fair to become useful and honorable members of society." When this article was written in 1876, the reformatory had in its charge a handful of girls and 100 or 120 boys between the ages of 8 and 18.

The boys did all the work of the institution, attended classes half-days, and participated in daily military drills. The older boys farmed, and any surplus produce as well as tinware made in the shops was sold.

Dr. Riheldaffer wrote of the value of "pleasurable excitement" in the lives of his charges. They were allowed celebrations and were excused from their studies and chores on holidays. "But we have one culminating bright period in our calendar, called the 'Minnesota State Reform School Annual Encampment,'" he said. Describing the week-long summer expedition, he wrote: "At last when the glad day comes all are in time, marching to the music of fife & drum, under the Stars and Stripes, seven miles away, on foot, to the camping ground, on the margin of one of our beautiful lakes."

Two of the pioneer reform school's structures are still in use on the campus of Concordia College. The Lutheran college purchased the reformatory property in 1894. The two yellow brick buildings, renovated and altered, are Old South at North Syndicate Street and Carroll Avenue (now a faculty office building) and Old West at 1270 Concordia Avenue (housing the music department). One of these was a reform school dormitory and classroom building; the other was the workshop where the boys did laundry, tailoring, shoemaking, and tinworking.

24 | Gibbs Farm Museum

2097 Larpenteur Avenue West

HEMAN GIBBS made a claim on this site in 1849 and built a shanty of logs and sod. The spot overlooked the Indian trail between Lake Harriet (in what is now south Minneapolis) and Forest Lake (north of present-day St. Paul) and was also on one of the earliest roads linking Minneapolis and St. Paul. In 1854 Gibbs replaced the sod shanty with a one-room, one-and-a-half-story frame house, and in 1867 he built the present structure, incorporating his one-room shack into its east end. Tamarack logs, which were used to strengthen the floor of the upstairs loft, still can be seen in the kitchen ceiling of the existing farmhouse.

The house has been attractively restored with some of the Gibbs family's original china and furnishings as well as other pieces typical of farmhouses of the 1860s and 1870s.

The red barn behind the house is an agricultural museum containing pioneer farm tools and machinery. Nearby stands a one-room rural schoolhouse dating from the 1890s which was moved to the Gibbs property from its original location in Chippewa County. The schoolhouse will be restored and furnished in a manner typical of the turn of the century.

The Gibbs Farm Museum is owned and maintained by the Ramsey County Historical Society. It is open to the public from May 1 to November 1 from 2:00 to 5:00 P.M. daily, except Mondays and Saturdays. From June 1 to September 1, the museum stays open until 8:00 P.M. on Wednesdays. Tours are given; groups may make reservations by calling the Gibbs Farm Home Museum.

MANY VISITORS tour the farmstead built by pioneer Heman Gibbs a century ago. The Ramsey County Historical Society acquired the property in 1949 to save it from destruction, and opened it as a museum in 1954. A grandson of Gibbs was present at the dedication. The barn, which contains displays of farm implements, was completed in 1959. Photograph by Becker, 1966.

25 | Muskego Church

On the campus of Luther Theological Seminary at Como Avenue and Luther Place

THE PULPIT and altar of Muskego Church were built by hand. Photograph by Becker, 1964.

THE FIRST CHURCH erected by Norwegian Lutherans in America has been preserved and now stands on the grounds of Luther Theological Seminary. It was built on a hill overlooking the community of Muskego, Wisconsin, near Milwaukee, in 1843–44 by a congregation which had previously met in various places. The members themselves supplied the labor, and most of the money for materials was contributed by friends in Norway.

The little church, with the addition of a chancel, served until 1869 or 1870, when it was sold to a farmer who used it as a barn. In 1904 it was rescued, dismantled log by log, and moved to its present location.

After it was reassembled, the exterior of "great oak logs, hewed flat on two sides" was covered with protective siding, and the interior was restored to its original simple appearance. The woodwork remains unpainted and unvarnished, with adz marks still visible; the pews are unpadded; and the seats in the small U-shaped gallery consist of planks mounted on sawhorses. The altar, the pulpit (which looks like the front of a chariot), the pedestal of the baptismal font, and the pillars supporting the gallery are of black walnut.

The church also contains an old pump organ, which was not among the original furnishings, and a wood-burning stove which the congregation acquired in 1849 after enduring five Wisconsin winters without heat.

Pictures of the first two pastors, lay leaders, and a circuit rider whose activities reached out from Muskego, as well as Bibles and other items, are on display.

The building, which is included in the National Historic American Buildings Survey, is open upon request at the seminary office. An informative marker was erected in 1963 by the Ramsey County Historical Society and the St. Paul City Planning Board.

THIS MARKER recording the history of Muskego Church is located on Luther Place near its junction with Como Avenue. Photograph by Becker, 1966.

22
MINNEAPOLIS LANDMARKS

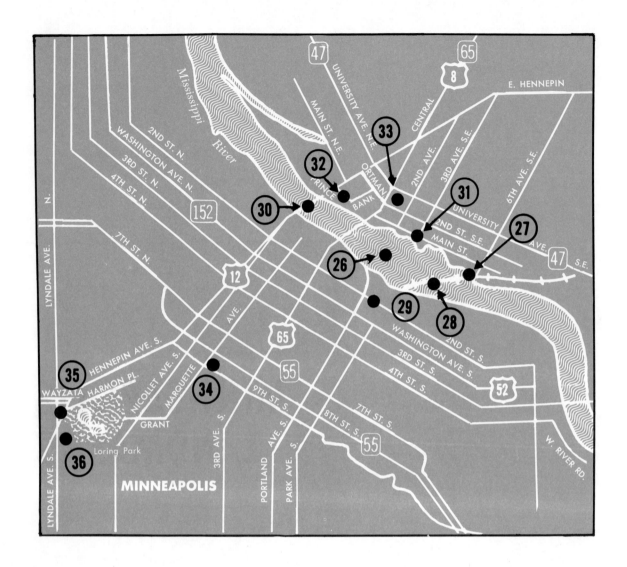

Downtown Minneapolis Area

Visible from the Third Avenue Bridge, the St. Anthony Falls Hydraulic Laboratory at the foot of Third Avenue Southeast, or the observation deck on the upper lock

THE PRESENCE of the Falls of St. Anthony, a broad, low waterfall in the Mississippi River, was probably the most important factor in the founding and growth of nineteenth-century Minneapolis.

Beside the falls in the years from 1821 to 1823 soldiers from newly established Fort Snelling (*see no. 48*) built a gristmill and a sawmill. Later the falls supplied the water power for the development of the city's two great pioneer industries — sawmilling and flour milling. In 1882 the falls powered the first hydroelectric central station in the United States.

Father Louis Hennepin (*see no. 35*) discovered and named the falls for his patron saint, Anthony of Padua, in 1680. The Indians of the area had given them such descriptive names as Kakabikah (the severed rock), Minirara (curling water), and Owahmenah (falling water), and had attached many legends to them. Hennepin saw an Indian in an oak tree weeping as he fastened to a branch a beaver robe decorated with porcupine quills — his sacrifice to the god of waters and evil dwelling beneath the falls.

After he returned to Europe Hennepin wrote a book, published in 1683, in which he described the falls. In 1778 Jonathan Carver published the earliest known sketch of the Falls of St. Anthony in one of the many editions of a book that became a best seller and spread the fame of the cataract throughout Europe.

A plaque erected by the United States Army Corps of Engineers, describing the geology of the falls and telling about events and structures in the vicinity, is located in the observation deck overlooking the upper lock. The deck may be reached by going north on Portland Avenue in Minneapolis to the Mississippi, ignoring the dead end sign, and continuing down the riverbank to the parking area near the Stone Arch Bridge. The platform is located in a yellow brick building to the right of the parking area; it is open daily from 8:00 A.M. to 10:00 P.M.

THE BEAUTY that made the Falls of St. Anthony famous has disappeared as locks and dams have been built to make the Mississippi navigable farther upstream. This is the Upper Harbor project, viewed from the west side. An observation deck is in the building in the center beyond the Stone Arch Bridge. Photograph by Alan Ominsky, 1965.

THIS is the first known picture of the Falls of St. Anthony. It appeared in Jonathan Carver's **Travels,** published in 1778.

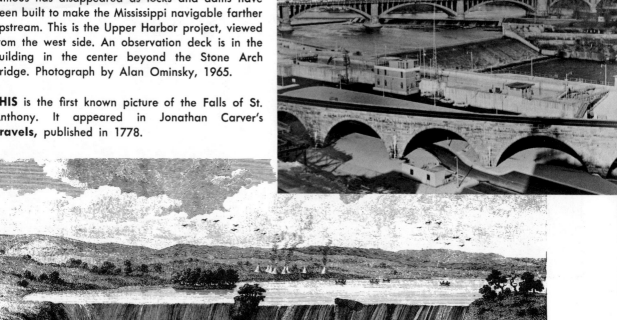

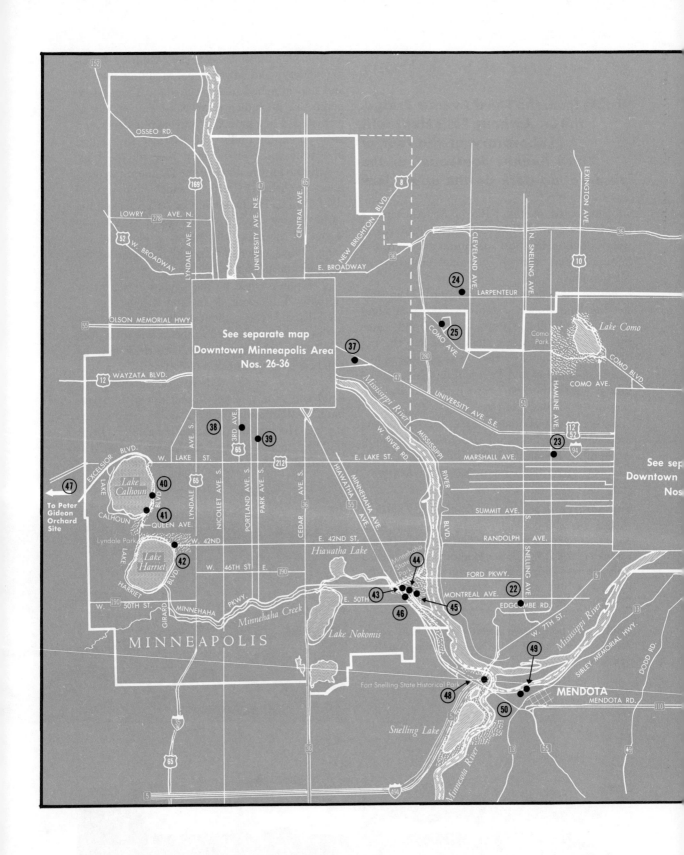

Twin City Historic Sites

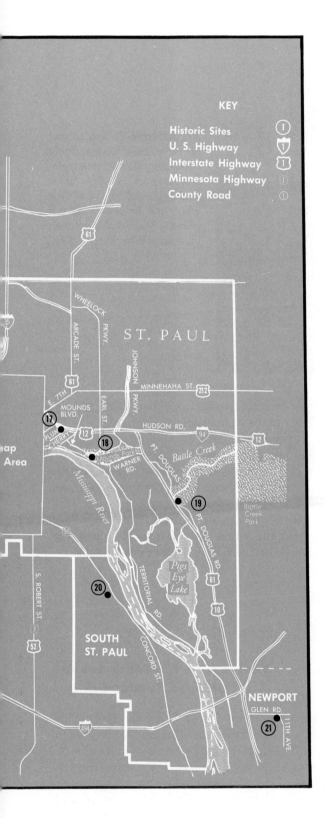

KEY

Historic Sites
U. S. Highway
Interstate Highway
Minnesota Highway
County Road

AN ARCHWAY and a boulder that once bore a tablet describing Father Hennepin's discovery of the Falls of St. Anthony mark the spot from which the Belgian friar supposedly viewed the cataract. Photograph by Becker, 1966.

27 | Lucy Wilder Morris Park

At the foot of Sixth Avenue Southeast

THIS TINY PARK, difficult to find and showing the results of many years of neglect, is nevertheless worth a visit. It marks the spot from which Father Louis Hennepin is thought to have seen and named the Falls of St. Anthony in 1680, and it affords an excellent view of the Stone Arch Bridge (*see nos. 26, 28, and 35*).

In 1924 a bronze tablet commemorating Father Hennepin's discovery was placed on the site by the Minnesota chapter of the Daughters of the American Colonists. The organization named the spot Lucy Wilder Morris Park in honor of its president. Sometime during the next ten years the bronze plaque was stolen. It was replaced, and again stolen in the 1960s.

When the marker was first installed in 1924, the land was owned by the St. Anthony Falls Water Power Company, one of the major developers of the falls. The area was leased to the city of Minneapolis in 1931 and later to the Hennepin County Historical Society, which in 1957 purchased the park for one dollar from the water-power firm, a subsidiary of Northern States Power Company. The society has since

suggested that the site might best be the responsibility of the Minneapolis park board.

At present the area is overgrown with weeds and shrubbery, and the falls, which have retreated upstream due to erosion since Father Hennepin saw them, are not visible from it. An iron archway marking the entrance to the park is barely discernible through the foliage just beyond the Great Northern tracks above the entrance to the Northern States Power plant.

28 | Stone Arch Bridge

Visible from the Tenth Avenue or Third Avenue Bridges

THE STONE ARCH BRIDGE below the Falls of St. Anthony is the result of "Empire Builder" James J. Hill's ambitious plan to improve railroad service to Minneapolis. In the 1880s when Hill announced his intention to build a bridge to accommodate the St. Paul, Minneapolis, and Manitoba Railway (later the Great Northern) lines serving Minneapolis, he said it would be the "finest structure of the kind on the Continent." He was right; a recent historical survey called it "one of the fine stone bridges in the nation."

Hill later recalled, however, that the construction of the span was "the hardest thing I ever had to do." When his plan was made public in 1881, a Minneapolis newspaper remarked: "This is regarded by our well-informed citizens as an utterly impracticable undertaking." Although the article expressed confidence in Hill's "honesty, sincerity, and the best of intentions," its first remark evidently expressed the sentiments of many people, for the project was immediately dubbed "Jim Hill's Folly."

The masonry structure, a rarity in the Midwest in those days and a complex engineering feat, was completed in 1883 at a cost of $690,000. The graceful span, which has been compared to a Roman aqueduct, is the oldest mainline bridge in the Northwest, and next to the Eads Bridge at St. Louis, the oldest railroad bridge over the Mississippi.

"It is a curious thing," Hill's biographer wrote, "that this bridge did more to advertise Mr. Hill's genius to the public of the Northwest than his [previous] great achievements. . . . Minneapolis was as yet a small city, but it was growing

wonderfully. The railroads east and west had to cross the river there or in the vicinity, and went over on the creaking wooden bridges so familiar to the Western pioneer. Mr. Hill looked ahead to the future of traffic, picked out the best place for a . . . station, and saw that the line of access most central and most convenient . . . required a bridge crossing at an angle just above the Falls of St. Anthony."

When "Jim Hill's Folly" became a successful reality, the local newspapers changed their tune. One called the "magnificent structure" a "fitting monument to the liberality, sagacity and enterprise of President Hill." With the completion of Hill's "grand" depot in 1885, the Empire Builder transformed railroad accommodations in Minneapolis.

The twenty-three-arch span served without major alteration or repair until 1962, when a pier and two arches near the west end were removed and replaced with a 196-foot steel span to allow river craft access to the lock near the foot of the Falls of St. Anthony. In 1965, for the first time in its eighty-two-year history, the Stone Arch Bridge was closed for emergency repairs made necessary by flood damage. It now carries a normal load of thirty passenger trains daily.

THE STONE ARCH BRIDGE sweeps across the Mississippi toward the Minneapolis milling district in this view taken in the early 1900s. At the west end is a tablet bearing Hill's name — an indication of his pride in this achievement. The tablet can be seen at the foot of Portland Avenue.

PHOTOGRAPHER Henry R. Farr sold stereopticon views of Minneapolis in the 1880s. This picture of the rebuilt Washburn A Mill was one he featured.

29 | Washburn A Mill

612 Second Street South

"THE NAME 'Minneapolis' has been carried around the world printed on the side of a flour bag or stenciled upon the head of a flour barrel," the Minneapolis Chamber of Commerce boasted in 1903. Indeed, from 1880 to 1930 Minneapolis was the flour-milling capital of the United States. The Washburn A Mill, which operated until July, 1965, was reputed in 1880 to be the largest mill in the United States and perhaps the biggest in the world.

This historic structure was built in 1879 by a group of partners that included Cadwallader C. Washburn, John Crosby, and William H. Dunwoody. It operated by water power supplied by the Falls of St. Anthony (*see no. 26*) and contained equipment which was to revolutionize flour milling — a middlings purifier and a new type of Hungarian roller. These innovations produced a superior grade of flour from the spring wheat grown in the west and north. Previously flour made from spring wheat had been inferior to that made elsewhere from winter wheat.

The Washburn A Mill that now stands on Second Street replaced an earlier mill of the same name. The present structure bears a plaque over the entrance telling a little of its story: "This mill was erected in the year 1879 on the site of Washburn 'A' Mill which was totally destroyed on the second day of May 1878, by fire, and a terrific explosion occasioned by the rapid combustion of flour dust. Not one stone was left upon another, and every person engaged in the mill instantly lost his life." Although fourteen men are named as victims on the tablet, a total of eighteen persons were killed.

The explosion, which local newspapers called a "terrible disaster," demolished not only the Washburn A but other nearby mills and businesses. It shattered windows up and down Washington Avenue and was felt as far away as St. Paul. Although it destroyed one-third to one-half of the city's milling capacity "at a stroke," an editorial in the *St. Paul Globe* on the following day expressed a well-founded optimism that Minneapolis would "arise from this fearful blow, and go forward even more brilliantly than before."

Within two months, most of the debris had been cleared away and plans for rebuilding the structures, including the "big mill," were under way. To prevent a recurrence of the disaster, dust collectors to eliminate the possibility of combustion were installed in the new mills.

The rebuilt Washburn A was twice the size of its predecessor. On June 30, 1880, the *Minneapolis Tribune* exclaimed: "Just Completed. The Largest and Finest Flouring Mill in the Whole World." Actually, on that date the mill was only half finished. By 1881, when all the equipment had been installed, the A's output exceeded 4,000 barrels a day.

The structure was seven stories tall, and had an attic topped by a cupola surrounded by a "piazza" for sight-seeing. It was built under the direction of William de la Barre, an engineer who was to become a prominent figure in the development of the water power at the Falls of St. Anthony.

32

30 | First Suspension Bridge

A few abutments remain under the Hennepin Avenue Bridge

THE MISSISSIPPI RIVER was bridged for the first time when a graceful suspension span was completed late in 1854 between Nicollet Island and the west bank. It met a bridge built three years earlier between the eastern shore and the island to form the first span to completely cross the Mississippi at any point.

In the early 1850s a journey from St. Anthony on the east bank to the newer and smaller settlement of Minneapolis on the west side was a "precarious and dangerous undertaking." During the winter, travel was simple enough on the ice, but when the ice broke up, pedestrians walked across a dam Franklin Steele had built to Nicollet Island, and then went the rest of the way in what was once described as "an imp of a boat that maliciously turned over on the slightest provocation."

The river between the communities was divided into two channels by Nicollet Island. Steele had begun a ferry service across the wider west channel in 1847 and had built a crude bridge over the east channel in 1851. By 1852 traffic was so heavy that this arrangement was inadequate. Leading residents of the area, among them Steele, Henry H. Sibley, Henry M. Rice, and John H. Stevens, formed the Mississippi Bridge Company. By the end of 1854 it was possible to cross the entire river via bridge.

The new span, which cost $36,000 to complete, was suspended between towers planted on Nicollet Island and the west bank. A St. Anthony newspaper described it as "the spider-like creation of a fairy of the Falls." Its opening was celebrated on January 23, 1855, with much ceremony. "There were music and banners . . . and when the first sleigh arrived at the bridge . . . cannon thundered forth" and the gates "were then thrown wide open." A party, composed of the "elite of St. Anthony, Minneapolis, Saint Paul and other places," crossed to Minneapolis, and then returned to St. Anthony, where a gala dinner was served, replete with numerous toasts — one of them to engineer Thomas M. Griffith who had designed the structure.

The bridge became a landmark. Travelers

WITH THE COMPLETION of this bridge, the Mississippi was spanned for the first time. The photo-graph was taken in 1855, the year the opening of the bridge was celebrated.

viewed it with interest, and local firms used sketches of it on stationery sent around the nation.

Tolls ranging from two cents for a sheep to twenty-five cents for a carriage were charged by the owners. The charges were reduced when Hennepin County purchased the span in 1867, and were abolished when St. Anthony and Min-neapolis merged in 1872 and took over the bridge.

The structure that had united the two towns was torn down in 1875 when it could not bear the increasing traffic. It was replaced by another suspension span built in 1875–76. That bridge was superseded in 1890 by the present steel-arch Hennepin Avenue Bridge.

31 | Pillsbury A Mill

Main Street and Third Avenue Southeast

AN ADVERTISEMENT appearing in 1905 read: "16,113 BARRELS OF FLOUR in one day, is the new record of the PILLSBURY A — the greatest mill in the world. No other TWO mills on earth can equal this record." The Pillsbury A was indeed one of the largest flour mills in the world at that time and for a number of years thereafter. For fifty years from 1880 to 1930 its capacity helped make Minneapolis the leading milling city in the United States.

The Pillsbury A was begun in 1879 by C. A. Pillsbury and Company. One of its two units was put into operation in 1881, the other in 1882. A massive gray limestone structure built at a cost of half a million dollars, it had seven stories "and an attic" and towered 112 feet above the ground. A flag flew from its top, and a great "A" loomed over the entrance. It was called the "most complete in all its appointments of the mills in Minneapolis," and it was "provided with every convenience that modern improvement can suggest." Powered by water from the Falls of St. Anthony and operated by two turbine engines of 1,200 horsepower each, it at first produced 4,000 barrels of flour daily. Later additions increased its capacity.

The Pillsbury A is of architectural as well as historical importance. It was designed by LeRoy S. Buffington, a Minneapolis architect who has been called the "Father of the Skyscraper."

THE PILLSBURY A MILL, completed in 1881, is still operating. This photograph shows the giant mill as it looked in 1886.

When it was built, the mill represented a departure from the Victorian style popular in the 1880s to a more functional design. "Much taste is exhibited in the elegance of its architecture and internal finish," remarked the *Minneapolis Tribune.*

As the oldest operating mill in the falls district, the Pillsbury A constitutes a link between the heyday of milling in Minneapolis and the present. It is listed in the National Historic American Buildings Survey. *It is not open to the public.*

32 | Our Lady of Lourdes Church

21 Prince Street Southeast

THIS PICTURESQUE landmark overlooking the Falls of St. Anthony is the oldest continuously used church in Minneapolis. It was built by the First Universalist Society of St. Anthony, of lime-

A ROMAN CATHOLIC congregation purchased and named Our Lady of Lourdes Church in 1877. These stairs replaced the original double-winding steps. Photograph by Gordon Ray about 1950.

stone quarried on Nicollet Island, at a cost of between $15,000 and $20,000. When it was dedicated on September 27, 1857, it was described as "unquestionably the most elegant house of worship in the Territory." Nearly five hundred people attended the ceremonies and heard a Chicago minister give three "eloquent and masterly" sermons.

The Universalists discontinued their use of the building in 1866 when their minister, the Reverend Seth Barnes, died. The society disbanded in 1869. In 1877 a French Catholic congregation arranged to purchase the property, and named the building Our Lady of Lourdes Church. The first mass was conducted by Father Pascal Brunelle on July 29. By that time only four members of the Universalist Society were left, and a special act of the legislature was required to make the transaction legal. It was passed in 1879.

The church soon proved too small for the new congregation, and in 1881 a transept, apse, sacristy, and quarters for the priest were added. The wooden Gothic steeple was built in 1882–83, and a new front entrance and a statuary niche were added in 1914.

Although it has been altered over the years and is now surrounded by the business and industrial area of southeast Minneapolis, this church is one of the city's few surviving pioneer structures. It is included in the National Historic American Buildings Survey.

33 | Ard Godfrey House

Richard Chute Square, University and Central Avenues

A SIMPLE, white frame house that is considered the oldest existing residence in Minneapolis stands all but forgotten in this little park.

The home was built in 1849 by Ard Godfrey in what was then the village of St. Anthony, the first settlement to grow up at the Falls of St. Anthony. It was originally located on a high bluff on Main Street Southeast, several blocks from its present site.

Godfrey was a millwright who came to the

Minnesota country from Maine in 1847 to construct the first commercial sawmill at the falls. It was to be built at a dam which Franklin Steele was erecting to harness the water power. When Godfrey arrived, he found that the dam had not been completed, and he was given the task of building both it and the mill. He successfully completed the two jobs in 1848.

Then he turned his attention to building a house so that his wife and children could come west to join him. The frame structure had a parlor, sitting room, dining room, bedroom, and a kitchen wing on the first floor, and four bedrooms on the second floor. Two fireplaces provided heat.

In May, 1849, the Godfreys' daughter Harriet was born in this house — the first white child to be born in what is now Minneapolis. Harriet later recalled that when she was a small child there were no hotels in St. Anthony, and "my mother entertained and lodged as many persons as she could find room for, accommodating many of them with beds on the floor."

Godfrey quickly became involved in many facets of village life — sawmilling, flour milling, water power, and real estate. In 1849 he served as St. Anthony's first postmaster, conducting the "mail department" in a corner of his lumber office.

Although he was later to return to the pioneer village, Godfrey moved in 1853 to a claim on Minnehaha Creek (now the property occupied by the Minnesota Soldiers Home), where he operated a sawmill until 1862. In that year he set out for the newly discovered gold fields of present-day Montana. He failed to strike it rich, but during his stay he built Montana's first sawmill. In 1863 Godfrey returned to Minnesota, where he lived until his death in 1894.

The neat house Godfrey built near the Falls of St. Anthony was moved to Chute Square in 1909. At that time the kitchen wing was removed.

The structure is owned by the Minneapolis Department of Parks and Public Recreation, and it is included in the National Historic American Buildings Survey. Although it was once operated as a museum by the Hennepin County Territorial Pioneers Association, *the house is not now open to the public.*

SCHOOL CHILDREN are shown visiting the Ard Godfrey House in this photograph taken about 1925, when the Hennepin County Territorial Pioneers Association maintained a museum there. Greeting them is Harriet R. Godfrey, the first white child born in what became Minneapolis. She died in 1943 at the age of ninety-three.

34 | The Foshay Tower

Ninth Street South and Marquette Avenue

THE FOSHAY TOWER is Minneapolis' tallest structure and its best-known landmark. It is one of the most unusual office buildings in the Northwest, and there is a bizarre story behind it.

The thirty-two-story tower was built in 1927–29 by Wilbur B. Foshay, who came to Minneapolis in 1915 with $200 in borrowed money, a practical education in utilities, and a desire to build an empire. In 1917 he formed the W. B. Foshay Company of Minnesota, and twelve years later he completed this monumental structure at a cost of nearly $4,500,000. At that time his utility company holdings, stretching across the United States and into Central America, were valued at $60,000,000.

The Foshay building has been characterized as "a symbol of . . . grandiloquent extravagance and the care-free wealth of the roaring 20's." When Foshay constructed the tower, he fulfilled a boyhood dream of building a structure similar to the Washington Monument in the nation's capital. A three-day dedication spree from August 30 through September 1, 1929, included fireworks, parades, and speeches. John Philip Sousa was there to lead his band in the "Foshay Tower Washington Memorial March," which he had written for the occasion. The governors of the forty-eight states and their wives were invited to the celebration, and Secretary of War James W. Good was present. The dedication cost the Foshay company nearly $127,000.

Two months later the stock market crashed, and the Foshay firm went into receivership. Foshay, the company's vice-president Henry Henley, and others were indicted for mail fraud. After two long trials, the suicides of a member of the first jury and her family, and other delays, Foshay and Henley were sentenced to fifteen years in Leavenworth Prison and fined a thousand dollars each.

THE FOSHAY TOWER was photographed by the Minneapolis firm of Norton and Peel in 1953.

Foshay went to jail on May 4, 1934, but three years later President Franklin D. Roosevelt commuted his sentence. He was released from prison in April, 1937. He lived in Colorado until 1952 and died in a Minneapolis nursing home in 1957 at the age of seventy-six.

A student of Foshay's career wrote, "Wilbur Foshay may have been innocent of deliberately intending to obtain investors' funds by a fraudulent scheme. Yet by building a holding company empire on a weak foundation, he had brought financial ruin to himself and thousands of investors." The lessons taught by the crash of Foshay's company and others like it were largely responsible for the subsequent passage of laws controlling utilities.

35 | Father Hennepin Statue

At the triangle formed by Hennepin Avenue South, Wayzata Boulevard, and Lyndale Avenue South

NEAR THE Basilica of St. Mary stands a statue of Father Louis Hennepin placed there in 1930 by the Knights of Columbus on the 250th anniversary of his discovery of the Falls of St. Anthony. (*See nos. 26 and 27.*) The statue is the work of sculptor Fred Slifer.

Father Hennepin was a Belgian friar of the Franciscan Recollect Order who went to New France in 1675. Four years later he accompanied La Salle's expedition to a fort on the Illinois River near present-day Peoria, and in the spring of 1680 with two other Frenchmen — Michel Ac-cault and Antoine Auguelle — he was sent to explore the upper Mississippi.

Ice hindered the party's progress up the river. Early in April, somewhere on the Mississippi at a point that has never been definitely established, the three were captured by a party of Sioux warriors. The men were taken to the large Indian village at Mille Lacs Lake, where they remained for about two months.

Hennepin found much to complain about during his sojourn with the Sioux. For example, when he was allowed to go with them on a canoe trip, he lamented that he was "continually employed in laving out Water, which soaked in again as fast as 'twas thrown out, through abundance of little Chinks. . . . It might have been properly said of this little Vessel, that when a Man was in it, he was in his Coffin; so crazy was it, and ready to break."

About July 1, Hennepin and one of his companions were permitted to go down the Mississippi to see if supplies from La Salle had arrived. "Our whole Equipage," Hennepin said, "consisted of fifteen or twenty Charges of Powder, a Fusil, a little sorry Earthen Pot, which the Barbarians gave us, a Knife between us both, and a Garment of Castor [beaver]. Thus we were equipt for a Voyage of 250 Leagues."

It was on this journey that Hennepin saw the only major cataract in the Mississippi River and named it for his patron saint, Anthony of Padua. He said the falls "of it self is terrible, and hath something in it very astonishing: However, it doth not come near that of Niagara."

Later that month, the explorer Du Luth, hearing that some white men had been captured by the Sioux, found Hennepin, Auguelle, and Accault (who had by then joined the hunting party), and accompanied them back to Mille Lacs, where he arranged their release.

In 1682 Hennepin returned to France. The following year he published a book about his adventures that made the Falls of St. Anthony a landmark in the vast wilderness of the midcontinent.

FATHER LOUIS HENNEPIN saw the Falls of St. Anthony in the wild and unexplored Minnesota country in 1680. This statue of the friar stands at a busy intersection in the city that now surrounds the waterfall. Photograph by Becker, 1966.

LORING PARK attracted children on a pleasant afternoon about 1900.

36 | Loring Park

Hennepin Avenue and Harmon Place

THIS PRETTY, thirty-six-acre park on the edge of downtown Minneapolis, where children and old-sters like to sit, walk, play, and feed the swans, was the first major tract acquired by the Min-neapolis park board. It was called Central Park until 1890, when it was renamed to honor Charles M. Loring, an early resident who was "active, zealous, and indefatigable" in his efforts to establish a comprehensive park system in the city.

Most of Loring Park was acquired in 1883, just after the citizens of Minneapolis voted to create a park board. Twenty years of debate over the value of parks and a bitter fight preceded the board's establishment. The city council op-posed the idea; the Knights of Labor said it would "open the way to fraud" and called it a "cunningly devised scheme by which the rich are to be made richer and the poor, poorer." In-stead the measure laid the foundations for the system of parks that is today the pride of Min-neapolis.

Charles Loring, a miller and merchant in the city, played a leading role in the creation of the board and served as its first president. He believed that "well considered plans for large public improvements . . . are profitable invest-

ments . . . invaluable to the health, the morals, and the pleasure of the people." This forward-looking man served for nine years as head of the board. During that time he spent a part of every pleasant day "in the field" with park employees.

Under his leadership and with the advice of Horace S. W. Cleveland, a landscape architect, Loring Park and others were developed. Cleve-land died in 1900, but his ideas greatly influ-enced the early development of the city's parks and boulevards. A marker extolling Cleveland's contribution and his "vision, reaching far beyond his time" was placed on his grave in Lakewood Cemetery in 1948.

Before Loring Park was landscaped, it was wild and hilly, with marshes and a spring-fed brook running through it. The area was even said to have "quagmires" and "bottomless pools."

In the days before white settlement of what is now Minneapolis, the park was crossed by an Indian trail leading from the Falls of St. Anthony to a Sioux village on Lake Calhoun. In the 1850s the land became the property of two farmers from Maine. In 1856 Joseph S. Johnson pur-chased what is now the southern part of the park and Allen Harmon bought the northern section. Both pioneers raised plentiful crops, and the largest of the lakes on the property (now Loring Lake) was known for many years by Johnson's name. A bronze tablet near the warming house marks the site of the Johnson farm.

After Loring Park was developed, a number

39

of other markers and monuments were placed there. They include Jacob Fjelde's statue of Ole Bull, a Norwegian violinist who gave concerts in Minnesota Territory in the 1850s, and a tablet honoring Maria L. Sanford, a beloved teacher at the University of Minnesota from 1881 to 1909.

THIS 1901 view of the University of Minnesota, taken from the Armory, shows (from left) Pillsbury Hall; Nicholson Hall (built in 1890 or 1891 and still in use); Eddy Hall; Burton Hall (erected in 1895 and still in use); and Old Main, which burned in 1904. Photograph by Sweet Studios, Minneapolis.

37 | University of Minnesota, Minneapolis Campus

The older area is on the east bank of the Mississippi River and is bounded on the north by University Avenue Southeast

ON A KNOLL across from Burton Hall on Pillsbury Drive stands a statue of John S. Pillsbury, a university regent (1863–1901) and governor of the state (1876–82). Erected in 1900, it is the work of Daniel Chester French, the sculptor of the quadriga on the State Capitol.

Pillsbury has fittingly been called the "Father of the University." When he began his long service as a regent in 1863, the institution was little more than a name. It had been chartered in 1851, but the financial panic of 1857, the Civil War, and the Sioux Uprising intervened, and by the time Pillsbury was appointed the university was sinking in a morass of debts and mortgages. His astute and vigorous action rescued the institution from threatened bankruptcy and saved most of the land to which the school was entitled under the federal land grant of 1851.

In 1869 Pillsbury presided at the inauguration of William Watts Folwell as the university's first president. At that time the school had a faculty of nine members, a freshman class of thirteen, and a preparatory department of about two hundred. Its first graduating class in 1873 numbered two young men.

A tablet in front of Shevlin Hall on Pillsbury Drive marks the location of the front entrance of Old Main, the first building erected on the campus. Begun in the late 1850s, Old Main was not completed until 1875. Portions of the structure burned in 1891 and 1892, and the entire building was destroyed by fire in 1904.

The oldest existing building on the campus is Eddy Hall, constructed in 1886 for use by mechanic arts classes. It stands at the intersection of Pillsbury Drive and Pleasant Street. A second structure dating from the 1880s is Pillsbury Hall at Pillsbury Drive and Church Street. It was erected in 1889 for use as a science building with funds given by Pillsbury. Both of these buildings were designed by LeRoy S. Buffington of Minneapolis, although the drawings for Pillsbury Hall were executed by his assistant, Harvey C. H. Ellis.

In 1908 the institution had about a dozen buildings, clustered casually around the knoll on the east bank of the Mississippi River. A competition was held to select a campus plan, and the winner was another famous Minnesota architect, Cass Gilbert, who also designed the present Capitol. The university has expanded far beyond the area Gilbert envisioned, but the central mall he designed remains an important feature.

38 | Hennepin County Historical Society and Museum

2303 Third Avenue South

AMONG THE DISPLAYS in the Hennepin County Historical Society's museum is one on "Main Street U.S.A.," a collection of eleven miniature buildings that might have constituted "Main Street" in the early 1900s. The exhibit, complete with dolls in period costume and thousands of tiny objects, is the work of the late Edna Knowles King, who spent many years making and assembling it.

Additional exhibits contain objects related to blacksmithing, a pioneer kitchen, a country store and post office, an early Hennepin County schoolroom, and other phases of the area's history.

The society also has a library as well as manuscript, autograph, picture, and print collections. The building is open to the public Tuesday through Friday from 9:00 A.M. to 4:30 P.M. and Saturday and Sunday from 2:00 to 4:30 P.M.

THE OFFICES AND MUSEUM of the Hennepin County Historical Society have been housed in this building since 1958. The English Tudor mansion was constructed by Minneapolis milling executive George C. Christian in 1919. Photograph taken in 1956.

THE MANSION built by Swan J. Turnblad now houses the American Swedish Institute. Among its visitors have been Dwight D. Eisenhower, Dag Hammarskjöld, Earl Warren, and members of the Swedish royal family. Photograph by Becker, 1966.

39 | American Swedish Institute

Park Avenue South and Twenty-Sixth Street

THE BUILDING that now houses the American Swedish Institute was built in 1907 at a cost of $1,500,000 as the home of Swan J. Turnblad, the owner of a Swedish-language newspaper, *Svenska Amerikanska Posten.*

Turnblad was born Sven Månson in 1860 in the province of Småland, Sweden. He immigrated to Vasa, Minnesota, with his parents when he was eight years old. His career with *Posten* began in Minneapolis when he was nineteen years of age. (It was about this time that he changed his name.) The newspaper was faltering, and Turnblad soon became the owner. Under his direction it became the largest Swedish-language newspaper in the United States.

One writer has suggested that the home Turnblad built, one of the grandest and most luxuriously furnished in the Northwest, probably was never intended for a dwelling, but as a testament and, possibly, as the achievement of the childhood dream of Sven Månson to own a castle. The building is a three-story, thirty-three-room architectural smorgasbord with towers, turrets, and terraces. Of gray limestone trimmed with turquoise, it is a massive, castlelike house surrounded by a high wrought-iron fence.

Turnblad and his wife and daughter traveled extensively, and when they were in Minneapolis they occupied only the second floor of the mansion. The family lived there just a short time. They found the house too large and handling the bevy of servants too difficult. Eventually they moved to an apartment across the street from which they could enjoy a view of the chateau.

The structure combines a "potpourri of details from many sources." Designed by architects Christopher Boehme of Minneapolis and Victor Cordella of Poland, it probably reflects the nineteenth-century trend toward the exotic in architecture as well as Turnblad's wish to build a show place exhibiting Scandinavian traditions and objects.

The interior is notable for its fine collection of eleven *kakelugnar* (or decorative porcelain stoves), its carved African mahoganies, its European furniture, and its Swedish rugs of Oriental design. One of the most outstanding features is a huge fireplace, faced in onyx with a ceiling-high mantel designed and carved by the noted Polish artist Albin Polesek. Another of the wood carvers represented in the mansion was Ulrich Steiner, a Swiss native who was so proud of his work that for fifty years he returned now and then to see it.

In 1929 Turnblad gave the mansion to the American Swedish Institute, which he had founded to foster Swedish culture in this country. Glassware, china, farm implements, and other objects are displayed in the institute, which is open to the public from 2:00 to 5:00 P.M. Thursday through Sunday. There is an admission charge.

40 | Pond Cabin Marker

On the east side of East Lake Calhoun Boulevard at approximately West Thirty-Fifth Street

TWO REMARKABLE young missionaries arrived at Fort Snelling aboard the steamboat "Warrior" on May 6, 1834. They were Samuel W. Pond, who was then twenty-six years old, and his brother Gideon H., twenty-four. They had made the long journey to the Minnesota country from Connecticut without a license or commission from any religious body but with an indomitable desire to bring Christianity to the Indians. Both were over six feet tall, and were described as "stalwart and sinewy, alert and genial."

They were welcomed to the frontier by the fort's commandant and by Indian agent Lawrence Taliaferro. The agent saw in the brothers a providential pair to supervise an agricultural experiment he had instituted among the Sioux of Chief Cloudman's band at Lake Calhoun.

The Ponds eagerly accepted Taliaferro's suggestion that they work at Cloudman's village, and by summer they had, with much difficulty, built a "good, snug little house, delightfully situated" on a spot the chief had selected because from it "the loons would be visible on the lake." Gideon later wrote: "That hut was the home of the first citizen settlers of Hennepin County, perhaps of Minnesota, the first school room, the first house for divine worship, and the first mission station among the Dakota [Sioux] Indians."

One of the brothers described the cabin as 12 by 16 feet in size and built of "carefully peeled" logs. He said, "Straight poles from the tamarack groves west of Lake Calhoun formed the timbers of the roof." These were covered with "the bark of trees which grew on the bank of a neighboring creek." Inside, a "partition of small logs divided the house into two rooms, and split logs furnished material for the floor. . . . The door was made of boards split from a log with an axe, had wooden hinges and fastenings. . . . The single window was the gift of the kind-hearted Major Taliaferro." The cash cost of the cabin was twelve and a half cents "for nails used about the door."

SAMUEL POND sent this map in a letter to his mother in Connecticut in 1834. He hoped the family would come west to visit the Lake Calhoun mission. This was probably one of the earliest maps of the future site of Minneapolis.

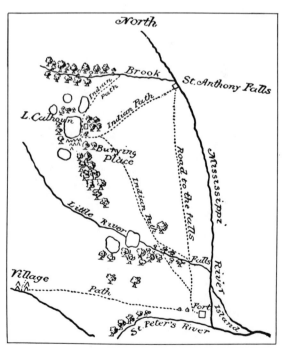

43

The Pond brothers labored long among the Sioux. One or both later served at Lake Harriet, Lac qui Parle, Shakopee, and what is now Bloomington. They are remembered for their pioneer work in devising a method of reducing the language of the Sioux (Dakota) to writing, for compiling a Dakota grammar and a dictionary, and for their valuable accounts of Indian life. Both eventually were ordained as Congregational ministers. Gideon died in 1878 at Bloomington; Samuel died at Shakopee in 1891.

The little house on Lake Calhoun stood only five years, and then was torn down by its builders "to get material with which to construct breastworks for the defense of the Dakotas after the bloody battle of Rum River." Nothing remains of the cabin, but a bronze plaque marks the site.

41 Cloudman's Village Marker

On the west side of East Lake Calhoun Boulevard at about West Thirty-Seventh Street

A TABLET near a busy boulevard — a spot now frequented by picnickers, swimmers, fishermen, and bicycle riders — "perpetuates the memory of the Sioux or Dakota Indians who occupied this

GEORGE CATLIN painted this oil of Cloudman's Village in 1835 or 1836. Photograph courtesy of the Smithsonian Institution, National Collection of Fine Arts.

region for more than two centuries prior to the treaties of 1851." Under the terms of those treaties, the Sioux relinquished all their Minnesota lands in exchange for payments from the government and a reservation on the upper Minnesota River.

The Sioux who lived on this site belonged to Cloudman's band to whom the famous missionary brothers, Samuel W. and Gideon H. Pond, came in 1834 (*see no. 40*). Although Cloudman was not a hereditary chief, he had been chosen by Lawrence Taliaferro, Indian agent at Fort Snelling from 1819 to 1840, as the most able man to lead this band.

According to Samuel Pond, Cloudman became convinced that his people should "turn their attention to agriculture" while he was hungry, out hunting in a snowstorm. After that he "tried to persuade others to adopt his views, but with no

success. It would have been well for the Dakotas," Pond wrote, "if they had had more chiefs like him, but he was far in advance of his contemporaries and was the only chief who was decidedly in favor of abandoning the chase and cultivating the arts of civilized life." The missionary described Cloudman as "a man of superior discernment, and of great prudence and foresight."

Taliaferro encouraged the band to farm, and supplied them with equipment and oxen. The Indians evidently had some measure of success, but they often lost their bean crop to pigeons and their corn to blackbirds.

Cloudman's village remained on this site until 1839 when the Indians moved to Oak Grove (Bloomington). A few years later Gideon built a home on the Minnesota River near the Indian camp.

42 | Lake Harriet Mission Schoolhouse Site

East Lake Harriet Boulevard and Forty-Second Street, across the street from the main beach

A FOUR-ROOM structure with loose boards for floors and partitions "not much better than none" was the first schoolhouse in what would become Minneapolis two decades later. It was built by two missionaries in 1836 on the east shore of Lake Harriet and was attended by Indian children and adults and by mixed-blood youngsters. (The tablet marking the site incorrectly gives the date as 1835.)

The builders were Jedediah D. Stevens, a Presbyterian minister, and Gideon Pond, a missionary who had begun his work with the Sioux at Lake Calhoun in 1834 (*see nos. 40 and 41*). Stevens persuaded Gideon and his brother Samuel that to be effective the missionaries must join forces, so they left their Lake Calhoun cabin, and during the next five years one or both of them stayed at Lake Harriet — teaching, studying Dakota (the Sioux language), or farming.

The missionaries erected both a school and a house at the Lake Harriet site. The house was

finished first, and in the summer of 1835 Stevens, his wife, his children, and his sixteen-year-old niece Cornelia settled there.

In 1835, before the schoolhouse was completed, Samuel wrote a "few simple lessons" and Cornelia began to teach the Indians to read and write Dakota. A few mixed-blood boys and girls, taken as boarders, were taught in English. In 1836 ten children were boarding, and there were also about ten or fifteen day students.

The missionaries found it difficult to keep the Indians in school. They were away for long periods on hunting expeditions, and they were "scared off easily" from their village by fear of the Chippewa.

In 1837 Cordelia Eggleston, Mrs. Stevens' sister, joined the mission to teach "the children of the forest," as she called the Indians. She and Samuel Pond were married in the schoolhouse in November, 1838. This was probably, as one writer put it, the "first marriage of white people in civilized form within the present limits of Minneapolis." The couple set up housekeeping in a small upper room of the school, where they lived without luxuries on Samuel's salary of two hundred dollars a year.

In 1839 the Sioux moved from the lake to a location less vulnerable to Chippewa attack, and the Lake Harriet mission was abandoned.

ONE OF MANY views of Minnehaha Falls, this painting was done by Robert S. Duncanson in 1862. It is in the Morgan Van Matre collection, Cincinnati.

43 | Minnehaha Falls, Minnehaha State Park

Accessible from Minnehaha Parkway or West River Road in Minneapolis or from Ford Parkway in St. Paul

THANKS to Henry Wadsworth Longfellow, Minnehaha Falls is one of the most widely known names in the entire state of Minnesota. The pretty fifty-three-foot cataract in present-day Minneapolis is also one of the state's oldest tourist attractions. It was visited by hundreds of nineteenth-century travelers long before Minnesota became a state and three decades before

Longfellow immortalized its "laughing waters" in *The Song of Hiawatha* published in 1855.

Soldiers from Fort Snelling explored Minnehaha Creek in the 1820s, and residents of the pioneer post often walked over the prairie to picnic near what they called Little Falls or Brown's Falls. Not until the late 1840s did it acquire the more poetic name "Minnehaha," meaning "laughing waters."

In 1835 artist George Catlin made his way to the upper Mississippi and returned to the East to "recommend to all who have time and inclination to devote to the enjoyment of so spendid a Tour, to wait not, but make it while the subject is new." He suggested that travelers take what he called a "Fashionable Tour" by steamboat up the Mississippi to Fort Snelling and then go to such scenic spots as Little Falls and the Falls of St. Anthony.

Catlin's suggestion caught on, and from the 1830s until the spread of railroad transportation after the Civil War, thousands of tourists made the trip. At first many of them were men, but a few women also ventured the hazards of such a journey. Among them was Elizabeth Schuyler Hamilton, the widow of Alexander Hamilton, a vivacious lady of eighty years who saw Minnehaha Falls in 1837. Artists, honeymoon couples, English authors, and parties numbering hundreds of people came via chartered steamboats or on regular excursions promoted by the steamboat companies.

These visitors not only painted the falls from every conceivable angle but also wrote about the cascade. Such new arrivals to Minnesota as Harriet E. Bishop, one of the area's early schoolteachers, added to the chorus. In a book published in 1857, Miss Bishop included a typical romanticized description of Minnehaha and its "melody of waters." "How beautiful the name, for it is a wild, *wild* laugh you hear," she wrote. "We part the foliage, and, standing upon the brink of a chasm . . . we behold the laughing waters, the whole width of the stream, making the bold leap. Nature speaks, and you are silent; but admiration is enthroned on the delighted countenance. . . . A small patch of blue is above us; the towering banks, with their gold and green foliage, are on the right and left; a perpendicular sheet of white spray is spread out before us, and behind us the roaring, tumbling stream hastens to the Mississippi."

By the Civil War era the fame of the falls had been carried far and wide by the visitors and by the appearance of Longfellow's poem. Ironically, the poet never saw the area. He based his description upon material collected and published by Mary H. Eastman in 1849 and upon a daguerreotype of the falls taken by Alexander Hesler in 1852. There is no record of a native legend involving an Indian maiden named Minnehaha, but the name apparently intrigued Longfellow, who created the romantic figure out of his imagination.

According to Longfellow, *The Song of Hiawatha* was "founded on a tradition prevalent among the North American Indians, of a personage of miraculous birth, who was sent among them to clear their rivers, forests, and fishing grounds, and to teach them the arts of peace."

The miraculous personage was known among the various tribes by several names, and Longfellow elected to use the Iroquois one, Hiawatha. Taking the story of the Iroquois chief Hiawatha as told by Indian agent Henry R. Schoolcraft, Longfellow wove into it many other curious legends celebrating the "land of the Dacotahs"

Where the Falls of Minnehaha
  Flash and gleam among the oak-trees,
Laugh and leap into the valley.

Not until 1875 was a park at Minnehaha Falls seriously suggested. Ten years later the Minnesota legislature authorized the purchase of the falls and its adjoining lands and the creation of a state park. In 1889 Minneapolis bought the still undeveloped land, and in the following years made improvements for the convenience of visitors. Although the city owns and maintains the area, it is still officially known as Minnehaha State Park.

44 | Hiawatha and Minnehaha Statue

In Minnehaha State Park

ACCORDING TO LONGFELLOW'S FAMOUS POEM, there dwelled in the "land of the Dakotahs" an ancient arrow maker and his "dark-eyed daughter."

With her moods of shade and sunshine,
  Eyes that smiled and frowned alternate,
Feet as rapid as the river,
  Tresses flowing like the water,
And as musical a laughter;
  And he named her from the river,
From the water-fall he named her,
  Minnehaha, Laughing Water.

The poem relates that Hiawatha passed by Minnehaha Falls, paused to purchase arrowheads from the maiden's father, and fell in love with Minnehaha. Later he returned to ask that she become his wife.

On an island above the falls stands a life-size bronze statue of Hiawatha and his bride Minnehaha. It depicts them journeying to Hiawatha's home, "the land of the Ojibways," to which Hiawatha bore the maiden in his arms "over wide and rushing rivers."

Erected in 1911, the statue is the work of Jacob Fjelde, a sculptor who came to Minneapolis from Norway as a young man in 1887. Among Fjelde's other works are statues of John H. Stevens (*see no. 45*), of Norwegian violinist Ole Bull (in Loring Park — *see no. 36*), and a bust of Norwegian dramatist Henrik Ibsen (in Como Park). His monument to the First Minnesota Regiment stands on the battlefield at Gettysburg.

Minneapolis school children donated more than a thousand dollars in pennies for the statue inspired by Longfellow's poem. It is perhaps the Twin Cities' best known piece of sculpture.

MINNEAPOLIS sculptor Jacob Fjelde created this statue of Minnehaha and Hiawatha in 1911.

45 | John H. Stevens House

In Minnehaha State Park

THIS SMALL white house was built in 1850 by the first permanent settler on the west bank of the Mississippi River in what is now Minneapolis. It was the home of John H. Stevens, a Canadian who had served in the Mexican War and worked in the lead mines of Wisconsin and Illinois before coming to the Minnesota country for his health in 1849.

Stevens, who had achieved the army rank of captain but was always addressed as "Colonel," received permission from the secretary of war to live on the then unsettled west bank. At the time the land was owned by the government as part of the Fort Snelling reservation, and Stevens was allowed to build there on the condition that he maintain a ferry for the crossing of troops.

In 1850 Stevens brought his bride to the little frame house, which originally stood on the riverbank below the present Great Northern Station. (A tablet at the southwest corner of the Railway Express Agency building at the foot of Nicollet and Hennepin avenues marks the original location of the dwelling.)

"During the last part of 1850 and the first part of 1851 we were alone on the west bank of the falls," Stevens wrote. "We have often gone to bed at night, within our homestead, waked up in the morning and seen that while all were asleep, the wigwams of either the Sioux, Chippewa or Winnebago, had gone up."

Stevens and his ferryman cleared the land and raised "bountiful crops" on the 160 acres he was allowed to claim. In the years from 1851 to 1854 other settlers joined him on the west bank, and in 1855 the government allowed them to buy the lands they had claimed.

Many significant events in the history of Minneapolis took place in this house. It was the scene of early political and religious meetings and court sessions and was a shelter for travelers. In this structure Indian chiefs and government agents met, Hennepin County was organized, the name "Minneapolis" was selected in 1852, and the first school district on the west side was established.

In all these events its genial owner played a prominent role. Stevens may truly be regarded as one of the founders of Minneapolis. He was associated with Franklin Steele in developing the water power of the Falls of St. Anthony, and he represented the area in the state legislature. For many years he also served as president of the Minnesota Agricultural Society.

Stevens died in Minneapolis in 1900 at the age of eighty, having lived to see the pioneer town he helped to found grow into a thriving city. His memory is perpetuated in a statue, the work of Jacob Fjelde, which stands near the house.

The Stevens house was moved several times. In 1896 it was towed to its present location in Minnehaha Park by nearly ten thousand school children working in relays. It is included in the National Historic American Buildings Survey.

46 | Minnehaha Depot

Between Hiawatha and Minnehaha Avenues at Forty-Ninth Street South

THE QUAINTLY ORNATE railroad depot near Minnehaha Park is a reminder of the Victorian era when gingerbread architecture was the order of the day, and bustled ladies and stiff-collared gentlemen traveled largely by rail. Today visitors reach Minnehaha Park by driving down busy city streets; ninety years ago the park was out in the country, and people went to it by train.

The Minnehaha station was on a line connecting Mendota and Minneapolis. The track was laid in 1865 by the Minnesota Central Railway Company, which had been known as the Minneapolis, Faribault, and Cedar Valley Railroad until the name was changed in 1864. Two years earlier this firm had taken over the rights and property of the Minneapolis and Cedar Valley road, the earliest ancestor of today's Milwaukee Road.

Incorporated in 1856, the Minneapolis and Cedar Valley began grading for a line from Minneapolis to Faribault in the late 1850s and

MINNEAPOLIS SCHOOL CHILDREN were granted a holiday on May 28, 1896, to move the John H. Stevens House to Minnehaha Park. They pulled it using long ropes, and teams of horses helped.

STATION AGENTS of the Milwaukee Road called Minnehaha Depot "the princess" because of its delicate architecture. Photograph by Becker, 1966.

49

early 1860s. When the Mendota-to-Minneapolis stretch was completed in 1865, the company ran what would now be called a suburban service. Between Minneapolis and Mendota there were three stations — South Minneapolis Junction, Minnehaha, and Fort Snelling.

The little wooden depot is thought to have been built in the mid-1870s. Throngs of picnickers and sight-seers took the train to the park, and others traveled to and from Fort Snelling and Mendota. In 1910 three trains of several coaches each made thirteen daily round trips to the park. Of these, eight carried passengers; the others only freight. Running time between Minneapolis and Minnehaha was sixteen minutes.

During World War I, the depot was a busy place because it handled shipments of supplies to Fort Snelling and served as a departure point for troops. It also did a big business in pre-World War II days handling the arrivals and departures of freight for the military post.

Later the depot was closed. In 1964 the Milwaukee Road presented the station to the Minnesota Historical Society, and the society's Transportation Museum Committee is restoring the structure to its original appearance. The interior has been refurbished, and the outside will be painted in the Milwaukee Road colors — yellow with red trim — which the depot wore in its active years.

47 | Peter M. Gideon Orchard Marker

Hennepin County Road 19, about one mile north of Minnesota Highway 7

ON THE SOUTHEAST CORNER of what was Peter M. Gideon's homestead is a marker commemorating this early Minnesota horticulturist's development of the Wealthy apple. Within view of the monument is the Gideon home, now more than a hundred years old, as well as the site of the orchards where he worked for forty-one years to produce hardy varieties of fruit.

Gideon and his wife, Wealthy, arrived in Minnesota from Ohio in 1853 and settled on the shores of Lake Minnetonka. In 1854 he began planting, seeding, and grafting fruit trees, but hard winters, blight, grasshopper plagues, and other reverses frustrated his efforts. At last in 1864 a seed obtained from Maine grew into a tree that survived the adverse conditions and the Wealthy apple was produced. This was the beginning of the Northwest's flourishing fruit-growing industry.

Gideon is also remembered for his crusading zeal on social issues. He condemned Negro slavery and the abuse of the Indians, supported women's rights, and fought for the "advancement of moral refinement."

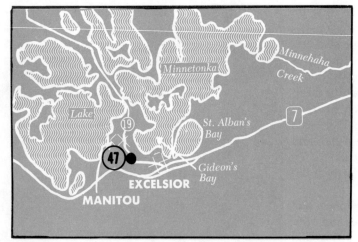

NO. 47 marks the site of the orchards where Peter M. Gideon developed the Wealthy apple.

3 LANDMARKS
FORT SNELLING
MENDOTA

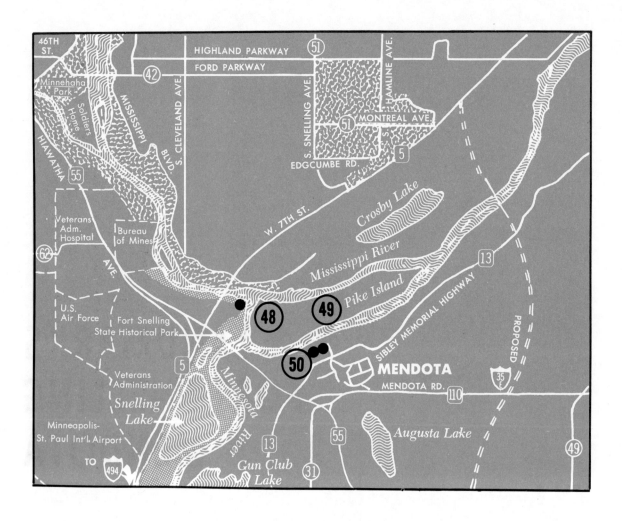

Fort Snelling—Mendota Area

48 . . . . . . Fort Snelling State Historical Park
49 . . . . Henry H. Sibley House
50 . . . . . . Jean Baptiste Faribault House

FORT SNELLING was pictured by artist J. C. Wild in gouache and pastels in 1844. The original is in the Minnesota Historical Society.

48 | Fort Snelling State Historical Park

Accessible from Minnesota Highways 5 and 55; the route is well marked

FORT SNELLING, established thirty-eight years before Minnesota became a state, is of major importance in the history of this area. It served as an outpost of civilization beyond the frontier, enforced peace among the Indians, extended the influence of the young United States over the region, and paved the way for white settlement. From its establishment in 1820 until Fort Ripley was built in 1849, Fort Snelling was the northwesternmost military post in the nation.

Lieutenant Zebulon M. Pike, for whom Pikes Peak was later named, selected the site of the future outpost at the junction of the Mississippi and Minnesota rivers in 1805, but fourteen years went by before Colonel Henry Leavenworth was sent to build it. He and his troops spent a terrible winter at Cantonment New Hope, a tem-

porary camp of log huts on low ground near present-day Mendota. In 1820 they moved to a more healthful location at Camp Coldwater on the west bank of the Mississippi and began the work of laying out the post.

Before much was done, Leavenworth was replaced in August, 1820, by Colonel Josiah Snelling. It was Snelling who selected the exact site of the fort on the scenic point between the rivers. He laid the cornerstone on September 10, 1820.

By 1824 Snelling had designed and supervised the erection of fifteen stone and wooden structures, laid out a parade ground enclosed by a stone wall, dug a well, and built at the Falls of St. Anthony a sawmill and a gristmill — the first mills in Minnesota (*see no. 26*). The post was at first called Fort St. Anthony, but the name was changed to Snelling in 1825.

Fort Snelling has been called "the cradle of Minnesota," and the distinction is deserved. The post was responsible for an impressive list of Minnesota "firsts." Within its walls the first school opened in 1823, and the first Protestant congregation was organized in 1835. There the area's first doctor ministered to the sick, and there, too, were founded the first hospital and the first circulating library. Its soldiers formed Minnesota's first band and put on its first theatrical productions. To Fort Snelling in 1823 went the "Virginia," the first steamboat to navigate the upper Mississippi. Soldiers from the fort were the first to use the water power of the Falls of St. Anthony. From the fort, too, came the first settlers of the state's two largest cities — Minneapolis and St. Paul. Within its walls the area's first post office opened in 1827, and the old post was the scene of early state fairs.*

As the area guarded by the pioneer post grew into a territory and then a state, the importance of the fort diminished. In 1858 it was closed, but with the outbreak of the Civil War in 1861 Fort Snelling was reoccupied. It remained an active army post until October 14, 1946. At that time it was turned over to the Veterans Administration, and the flag was lowered for the last time over

*Additional information on the post is attractively presented in booklet no. 1 of the Minnesota Historic Sites Pamphlet Series, published by the Minnesota Historical Society. Entitled *The Story of Fort Snelling*, it is illustrated with cartoons by Kern O. Pederson.

a fort which had served the nation for 126 years.

Agitation to preserve Fort Snelling as one of Minnesota's most significant landmarks began in the nineteenth century, but it was not until the 1930s that any concrete steps were taken. By then, time and changing use had taken their toll, and only the first road and four of the original structures remained — the Round Tower, the Hexagonal Tower, the Officers' Quarters, and the Commandant's House — the oldest buildings in the state. Of these the Hexagonal Tower most closely resembled the structure Snelling built; the other three had been greatly changed.

In the 1930s the Round Tower was made into a museum. Nothing more was done until 1957–58 when the Minnesota Statehood Centennial Commission sponsored an archaeological investigation that located the foundations of the wall and seven more buildings. In 1960 the old fort was designated as a National Historic Landmark; in 1961 the Minnesota legislature created Fort Snelling State Park. Four years later the legislature appropriated the first funds to begin the long-range project of restoring the old fort. Visitors to the park can see the exteriors of the existing buildings, watch the restoration work in progress, and view the foundations exposed thus far. The park is open daily.

49 | Henry H. Sibley House, Mendota

North of Minnesota Highway 13, accessible from Minnesota Highways 110 and 55

ONE OF THE best-preserved and historically significant spots in the state is the village of Mendota, the first permanent white settlement in what became Minnesota. Here stand the Sibley House — the oldest existing private home in the state — the Jean B. Faribault and the Hypolite Du Puis houses, and St. Peter's Catholic Church, which is more than a century old (*see no. 50*).

When Colonel Henry Leavenworth arrived in the Minnesota country in 1819 to establish a

military post at the confluence of the Mississippi and Minnesota rivers, he camped on the future site of Mendota, calling it Cantonment New Hope (*see no. 48*). After Fort Snelling was built, a fur trade center and a settlement grew up near the location of the old cantonment. At first it was known as New Hope or St. Peter's, but in the 1840s it became Mendota, a Sioux word meaning "meeting of the waters."

In 1834 Henry H. Sibley, a twenty-three-year-old trader for the American Fur Company, arrived at the mouth of the Minnesota River. From that time until his death in 1891, this man played a leading part in Minnesota's development. Many years later Sibley recalled: "When I first caught a glimpse of Fort Snelling, and descended the hills to Mendota, then called St. Peters, I little anticipated that the hamlet was to be my abiding place for 28 years. There were

THE HENRY H. SIBLEY House at Mendota today looks much as it did when this photograph was taken in the 1920s.

a few log houses at St. Peters, occupied by persons employed in the fur trade."

In 1835 Sibley built the stone house which became his home. It was constructed of limestone blocks cemented with mud from the riverbanks. The interior walls and ceilings were made of grasses and willow branches woven together by Sioux women and then plastered with mud. The beams, floors, and window sills were fashioned of hand-hewn timbers fitted with wooden pegs.

Sibley maintained a bachelor residence in the house for eight years, managing the fur trade of a region larger than the present state. He conducted his business and operated a trading store in the large front room on the first floor of the house. An outside stairway led to the attic, which was always available to Indians who needed shelter.

The trader described his life during this period in a letter to his sister: "If I should tell you that I milk my own cows, make my own pickles, wash my own dishes & make my own butter, I should . . . be telling no fibs. . . . I shall not satisfy your curiosity by telling you that my house is kept in good or bad order, clean or filthy or whether I do or do not frequently have half a score of cleanly Indians stretched out for the night upon my floor."

After 1843 when Sibley married Sarah Jane Steele — the sister of Franklin Steele, who was later a founder of St. Anthony — the house became more elegant. Sibley's office was moved to a new wing, and another addition at the rear provided more space for the family, which eventually included nine children and often Mrs. Sibley's mother, sisters, and various other guests. When Alexander Ramsey arrived to assume the governorship of newly organized Minnesota Territory in 1849, he, his wife, and his infant son were the Sibleys' guests for a month. It was from the Sibley home that Ramsey issued the proclamation declaring Minnesota Territory officially organized on June 1, 1849.

The tall, darkly handsome man who built this house had a long and distinguished career. He served as Minnesota's first delegate to Congress, and it was he who secured passage of the act creating the territory. He was the first justice of the peace in a vast area comprising parts of Iowa, the Dakotas, and all of what is now Minnesota west of the Mississippi. He helped frame the state Constitution, and he was the first elected governor (1858–60). He led the troops in the Sioux Uprising of 1862, and he devoted his life to civic and business pursuits in his adopted state.

The Sibleys moved to St. Paul in 1862. The Mendota house was subsequently used as a parochial school, an art school, a warehouse, and finally was abandoned. In 1910 the Sibley House Association, an organization of the Minnesota Daughters of the American Revolution, opened the house to the public. It was restored and refurnished, and it contains mementos of the Sibleys' residence there. It is open from May 1 to October 31, Tuesdays through Saturdays from 10:00 A.M. to 5:00 P.M. and on Sundays and holidays from 1:00 to 6:00 P.M. There is an admission charge; guided tours are offered.

Hypolite Du Puis House

At Mendota, southeast of the Sibley House

THIS brick house was built in 1854 by Hypolite Du Puis, who was Sibley's private secretary for many years. It is now operated as a tearoom by the DAR, and it has been enlarged and modernized over the years. Lunches and dinners are served between noon and 7:00 P.M. during the summer.

St. Peter's Catholic Church

On Minnesota Highway 13, adjacent to the Sibley and Faribault Houses

ON A HILL south of the Sibley House stands St. Peter's Catholic Church, the oldest such building in continuous use in the state. It was built in 1853 of limestone quarried nearby. Three earlier structures had been used by Mendota Catholics: a log cabin given by Jean Faribault, Faribault's own stone house, and a wooden chapel constructed during Father Lucien Galtier's years at Mendota. The exterior of the church erected during Father Augustin Ravoux's pastorate looks today much as it did in 1853, although the steeple has been replaced twice. The interior has been altered.

56

50 | Jean B. Faribault House

At Mendota, next door to the Sibley House

PIONEER, fur trader, friend of the Indians, and befriender of missionaries, Jean Baptiste Faribault led an exciting, arduous, and often perilous life in this region for half a century before Minnesota Territory was established. Respected by Indians and whites alike, he was described as being a small man "of prepossessing appearance, of much dignity, frankness, affability and urbanity of manner."

Faribault was born in what is now Canada. In 1798, when he was in his early twenties, he joined the North West Company as a fur trader. For ten years he conducted his business primarily from Michilimackinac (Michigan), but he may have been in the Minnesota country before 1800. In 1809 he began trading independently at Prairie du Chien (Wisconsin).

About 1819, at the urging of Colonel Henry Leavenworth, who was "much impressed" with his "intelligence and extensive knowledge of the Sioux Indians, their character and habits," Faribault and his family moved to Pike Island at the junction of the Mississippi and Minnesota rivers. Their dwelling was flooded, and they relocated on the east bank of the Mississippi. After that home was also flooded in 1826, the Faribault family settled at Mendota.

The colonial-style stone house preserved at Mendota was probably built in 1839 or 1840. Its construction is similar to that of the Sibley House (see no. 49). Faribault maintained lovely gardens and orchards, and his home became something of a community center — the third floor had a large room that was used as a ballroom and meeting hall.

An ardent Catholic, Faribault offered lodging to Father Lucien Galtier when he came to Mendota in 1840 and to his successor, Father Augustin Ravoux. For a brief period in 1842 Faribault's house served as a chapel.

After the death of his wife in 1847, the old gentleman moved to Faribault, the Minnesota town named for his oldest son, Alexander. For a time Jean Baptiste's grandson George operated the Mendota house as a hotel; later it was rented, used as a storehouse, and finally deserted.

In 1934 federal agencies, the Daughters of the American Revolution, and the Minnesota High- way Department began to restore the building. It was deeded to the DAR and was opened to the public in 1937. It now serves as a meeting place for the organization and as a museum of Indian artifacts; it is open from May 1 to No- vember 1 during the same hours as the Sibley House. There is an admission charge, and tours are offered.

FUR TRADER Jean B. Faribault built this house with local materials about 1840. At that time, Faribault had lived at Mendota for some years. Photograph 1959, courtesy National Park Service.

Selected Bibliography of Source Materials

The FOLLOWING BOOKS, manuscripts, and newspapers were most useful in compiling this booklet. All may be found in the collections of the Minnesota Historical Society.

BOOKS, ARTICLES, AND PAMPHLETS

Atwater, Isaac, ed., *History of the City of Minneapolis, Minnesota* (New York, 1893).

Bisbee, Herman, *Memoir of Rev. Seth Barnes* (Cincinnati, 1868).

Blegen, Theodore C., "The 'Fashionable Tour' on the Upper Mississippi," in Rhoda R. Gilman and June Drenning Holmquist, eds., *Selections from "Minnesota History": A Fiftieth Anniversary Anthology*, 72–82 (St. Paul, 1965).

———, "The Pond Brothers," in *Minnesota History*, 15:275–281 (September, 1934).

Bushnell, David I., Jr., *Villages of the Algonquian, Siouan, and Caddoan Tribes West of the Mississippi* (Smithsonian Institution, Bureau of American Ethnology, *Bulletins*, no. 77 — Washington, 1922).

Carver, Jonathan, *Travels Through the Interior Parts of North-America* (London, 1778).

Chicago, Milwaukee, St. Paul and Pacific Railroad Company, *Brief Record of the Development of The Milwaukee Road From the Chartering of its First Predecessor Company in February 1847 to Date — July 1944* ([Chicago, 1944]).

Christison, Muriel B., "LeRoy S. Buffington and the Minneapolis Boom of the 1880's," in *Minnesota History*, 23:219–232 (September, 1942).

Crooks, William, "The First Railroad in Minnesota," in *Minnesota Historical Collections*, v. 10, part 1, p. [445]–448 (St. Paul, 1905).

Culligan, John M., and Harold J. Prendergast, "St. Joseph's Hospital in St. Paul," in *Acta et Dicta*, 6:[195]–200 (October, 1934).

Dean, William B., "A History of the Capitol Buildings of Minnesota, With Some Account of the Struggles for Their Location," in *Minnesota Historical Collections*, 12:[1]–42 (St. Paul, 1908).

Dupre, Huntley, ed., "E. D. Neill's Gospel of Minnesota," in *Minnesota History*, 30:208–210 (September, 1949).

Edgar, William C., *The Medal of Gold* (Minneapolis, 1925).

Engebretson, Betty L., "The House that Mr. Stevens Built," in *Gopher Historian*, 1–7 (Spring, 1966).

Ferguson, Franklin T., "The Cathedral of St. Paul," in *Minnesota History*, 39:153–162 (Winter, 1964).

Folsom, Merrill E., *Great American Mansions and Their Stories*, 267–275 (New York, 1963).

Folwell, William W., *A History of Minnesota*, v. 1 (revised edition, St. Paul, 1956); v. 3 (St. Paul, 1926).

[Great Northern Railway Company], *The Autobiography of an Engine: The Story of the William Crooks and its Big Brother No. 2500* (n.p., [1923]).

Hart, Irving H., "The Story of Beengwa, Daughter of a Chippewa War Chief," in *Minnesota History*, 9:319–324 (December, 1928).

Heilbron, Bertha L., "Some Sioux Legends in Pictures," in *Minnesota History*, 36:18–23 (March, 1958).

Hennepin, Louis, *A New Discovery of A Vast Country in America* (London, 1699).

Hobart, Chauncey, *History of Methodism in Minnesota* (Red Wing, 1887).

———, *Recollections of My Life: Fifty Years of Itinerancy in the Northwest* (Red Wing, 1885).

Hodge, Frederick W., ed., *Handbook of American Indians*, v. 1 (Smithsonian Institution, Bureau of American Ethnology, *Bulletins*, no. 30 — Washington, 1907).

Holmquist, June D., and Jean A. Brookins, *Minne-*

sota's Major Historic Sites: A Guide (St. Paul, 1963).

Hurley, Sister Helen Angela, On Good Ground: The Story of the Sisters of St. Joseph in St. Paul (Minneapolis, 1951).

———, "The Sisters of St. Joseph and the Minnesota Frontier," in Minnesota History, 30:1–13 (March, 1949).

Johnson, Richard W., "Fort Snelling from its Foundation to the Present Time," in Minnesota Historical Collections, 8:[427]–448 (St. Paul, 1898).

Fridley, Russell W., "Fort Snelling: From Military Post to Historic Site," in Minnesota History, 35:178–190 (December, 1956).

Kane, Lucile M., The Waterfall That Built A City: The Falls of St. Anthony in Minneapolis (St. Paul, 1966).

———, "First Bridge over the Mississippi," in Gopher Historian, 13–16 (Spring, 1964).

Koeper, H[oward] F., Historic St. Paul Buildings: A Report of the Historic Sites Committee, a special citizens group named by the St. Paul City Planning Board (St. Paul, 1964).

Kuhlmann, Charles B., The Development of the Flour-Milling Industry in the United States With Special Reference to the Industry in Minneapolis (Boston, 1929).

Longfellow, Henry W., The Song of Hiawatha (Boston, 1855).

Loring, Charles M., "History of the Parks and Public Grounds of Minneapolis," in Minnesota Historical Collections, 15:[599]–607. (St. Paul, 1915).

Mattocks, John, "The Life and Explorations of Jonathan Carver," in Minnesota Historical Collections, 2:[266]–284 (St. Paul, 1889).

Minnesota Outdoor Recreation Resources Commission with the Minnesota Historical Society, Fort Snelling (Minnesota Outdoor Recreation Resources Commission, Reports, no. 15 – St. Paul, 1965).

Mizener, Arthur [M.], The Far Side of Paradise: A Biography of F. Scott Fitzgerald (Boston, 1951).

"Muskego Church," in Minnesota History, 38:231–233 (March, 1963).

Peabody, Lloyd, "History of the Parks and Public Grounds of St. Paul," in Minnesota Historical Collections, 15:[609], 620 (St. Paul, 1915).

Pederson, Kern O., The Story of Fort Snelling (Minnesota Historic Sites Pamphlet Series – St. Paul, 1966).

Pond, S[amuel] W., Jr., Two Volunteer Missionaries Among the Dakotas or The Story of the Labors of Samuel W. and Gideon H. Pond (Boston and Chicago, 1893).

Potter, Alan H., "Minnesota's Most Famous Spot: Minnehaha Falls," in Gopher Historian, 8–13 (Spring, 1965).

Pyle, Joseph G., The Life of James J. Hill, v. 1 (New York, 1917).

Randall, John H., "The Beginning of Railroad Build-

ing in Minnesota," in Minnesota Historical Collections, 15:[215]–220 (St. Paul, 1915).

Riggs, Stephen R., Tah-Koo Wah-kan; or, The Gospel among the Dakotas (Boston, 1869).

Shutter, Marion D., ed., History of Minneapolis: Gateway to the Northwest, v. 1 (Chicago and Minneapolis, 1923).

Sibley, H[enry] H., "Reminiscences; Historical and Personal," in Minnesota Historical Collections, 1:[374]–396 (St. Paul, 1902).

———, "Memoir of Jean Baptiste Faribault," in Minnesota Historical Collections, 3:[168]–179 (St. Paul, 1880).

———, "Reminiscences of the Early Days of Minnesota," in Minnesota Historical Collections, 3:[242]–282 (St. Paul, 1880).

State of Minnesota, Department of Administration et al., The Minnesota Capitol: Official Guide and History ([St. Paul], 1963).

Stevens, John H., Personal Recollections of Minnesota and Its People, and Early History of Minneapolis (Minneapolis, 1890).

Swanson, Roy [W.], "Frontiermen of Minnesota," in American Swedish Monthly, v. 42, no. 6, p. 84, 85, 87 (June, 1948).

Torbert, Donald R., Historical Survey I: A survey of buildings and structures of historic and architectural significance in the Central and Powderhorn Communities (Urban Design Study, Community Improvement Program, Background Reports, no. 3 – Minneapolis, 1965).

Turnbull, Andrew, Scott Fitzgerald (New York, 1962).

United States Army Corps of Engineers, St. Paul District, "St. Anthony Falls Upper Harbor Project: Mississippi River, Minneapolis," (St. Paul, 1960).

Upham, Warren, Minnesota Geographic Names: Their Origin and Historic Significance (Minnesota Historical Collections, 17:80, 438, 439, 443 – St. Paul, 1920).

———, and Rose B. Dunlap, comps., Minnesota Biographies (Minnesota Historical Collections, v. 14 – St. Paul, 1912).

Upjohn, E[verard] M., Buffington and the Skyscraper, reprinted from The Art Bulletin, v. 17 (New York, [1935]).

Williams, J. Fletcher, A History of the City of St. Paul, and of the County of Ramsey, Minnesota (St. Paul, 1876).

———, "Henry Hastings Sibley: A Memoir," in Minnesota Historical Collections, 6:[257]–310 (St. Paul, 1894).

——— et al., "Tributes to the Memory of Rev. John Mattocks," in Minnesota Historical Collections, 3:[304]–313 (St. Paul, 1880).

[Wirth, Theodore], Retrospective Sketch of the First Half-Century of Minneapolis Park Development under the Board of Park Commissioners 1883–1933 ([Minneapolis, 1933]).

MANUSCRIPTS

The papers of Ard Godfrey, Gideon H. and Samuel W. Pond, John G. Riheldaffer, Alexander Ramsey, and Henry H. Sibley were valuable. These and those below are in the manuscripts collection of the Minnesota Historical Society.

Long, Stephen H., "Journal from Prairie du Chien to the Falls of St. Anthony," [1817], Long Papers.

McNulty, Marcy F., "Wilbur Burton Foshay: The Saga of a Salesman," Creighton University (Omaha) masters thesis, 1964.

Minnesota Railroad and Warehouse Commission, "Analysis of Construction History and Gratuities Received by the Nineteen (19) 'Original Railroad Construction Entities' Comprising the Present (1917) Railroad Instrumentality Operated by the 'Chicago, Milwaukee & St. Paul Railway Company' in Minnesota."

St. Croix Valley Old Settlers Association Papers. Of special interest is the biographical sketch of Jacob Fahlstrom in the "Obituary Record."

Wilson, Quintus C., "Joseph Albert Wheelock: A Study of his Life and of the Impact of his Editorial Direction in St. Paul, Minnesota and the Northwest," University of Minnesota Ph.D. thesis, 1953.

Works Project Administration, Minnesota, Papers, especially the Historic Buildings Survey.

NEWSPAPERS

Daily Globe (St. Paul), May 3, 1878, p. 1, "Death and Destruction," and [2], editorial, "An Appalling Calamity"; May 4, 1878, p. 1, "The Disaster," all on the Washburn A Mill explosion.

Daily Pioneer Press (St. Paul), June 3, 1907, p. 1–5, 7, 8, "Archbishop Ireland Lays Cathedral Cornerstone," on the Cathedral of St. Paul.

Daily Minnesota Tribune (Minneapolis), January 7, 1883, p. 4, editorial, "The Great Blockade Raised," on the Stone Arch Bridge and the union terminal; August 10, 1883, p. 6, "The Stone Arch Bridge."

St. Anthony Express (St. Anthony Falls), January 13, 1855, p. [2], "Address of John H. Stevens, Esq.," recollections of St. Anthony since its founding.

Tribune (Minneapolis), May 3, 1878, p. 1, "The Explosion" and "A Record of Terror," and p. [4], "Like A Besom," all on the Washburn A Mill explosion; May 16, 1880, p. 5, editorial, "The Iron Ways," on railroads and the union depot, and 6, "Mammoth Improvements," on railroads and water power facilities in Minneapolis; June 30, 1880, p. 6, "Just Completed" on the Washburn A Mill; May 15, 1881, p. 9, 11, "Milling Metropolis." Also see mill firm advertisements in this issue on pages 10–15, 24.

Index